TRANSFORMATIVE LEARNING FOR SOCIAL WORK

TRANSFORMATIVE LEARNING FOR SOCIAL WORK

LEARNING FOR AND IN PRACTICE

EDITED BY

CLARE STONE WITH FIONA HARBIN

Selection and Editorial Matter © Clare Stone and Fiona Harbin 2016
Individual chapters © contributors 2016

All rights reserved. No reproduction, copy or transmission of this publication may be made without written permission.

No portion of this publication may be reproduced, copied or transmitted save with written permission or in accordance with the provisions of the Copyright, Designs and Patents Act 1988, or under the terms of any licence permitting limited copying issued by the Copyright Licensing Agency, Saffron House, 6–10 Kirby Street, London EC1N 8TS.

Any person who does any unauthorized act in relation to this publication may be liable to criminal prosecution and civil claims for damages.

The authors have asserted their rights to be identified as the authors of this work in accordance with the Copyright, Designs and Patents Act 1988.

First published 2016 by
PALGRAVE

Palgrave in the UK is an imprint of Macmillan Publishers Limited, registered in England, company number 785998, of 4 Crinan Street, London, N1 9XW.

Palgrave Macmillan in the US is a division of St Martin's Press LLC, 175 Fifth Avenue, New York, NY 10010.

Palgrave is a global imprint of the above companies and is represented throughout the world.

Palgrave® and Macmillan® are registered trademarks in the United States, the United Kingdom, Europe and other countries.

ISBN 978–1–137–54235–9 paperback

This book is printed on paper suitable for recycling and made from fully managed and sustained forest sources. Logging, pulping and manufacturing processes are expected to conform to the environmental regulations of the country of origin.

A catalogue record for this book is available from the British Library.

A catalog record for this book is available from the Library of Congress.

Printed and bound in Great Britain by CPI Group (UK) Ltd, Croydon, CR0 4YY

CONTENTS

List of Illustrations — x
Contributors — xii
Acknowledgements — xv

Introduction — 1
Clare Stone and Fiona Harbin

    How You May Use This Book — 8
    How the Book is Structured — 9

1 The Transition from Student to Practitioner: Managing the Social Work Learning Journey — 11
Fiona Harbin

    Introduction — 11
    Key Points — 13
    Significance for Social Work Practice — 13
    Using in Practice — 15
    Self-Assessment Audit Tool: Skills and Knowledge — 18
    Conclusion — 23

2 Embedding the Principles of Adult Learning — 24
Clare Stone

    Introduction — 24
    Key Points — 25
    Significance for Social Work Practice — 25
    Using in Practice — 30
    Behaviour Modification — 31
    Cognition Within Learning — 32
    Constructive Alignment — 33
    Learning Taxonomy — 34
    Learning Styles — 35
    Modelling — 37
    Card Sort — 38
    Other Mediums for Supporting Learning — 40
    Reflective Supervision as Learning Methodology — 41

Recording Learning	42
Learning Agreement/Learning Contract for Learning in the Workplace	43
Career Development and Career Advancement	45
Acknowledging Challenges to Learning	48
Conclusion	49

3 Fostering Emotional Intelligence Within Social Work Practice — 50
Clare Stone

Introduction	50
Key Points	51
Significance for Social Work Practice	51
Using in Practice	53
Knowing Oneself	57
Self-efficacy	60
Developing Emotional Intelligence in Supervision	63
Conclusion	63

4 Developing Resilience for Effective and Safe Practice — 65
Clare Stone

Introduction	65
Key Points	65
Significance for Social Work Practice	66
Using in Practice	67
Bolstering Confidence	72
Building Resilience: Identifying and Managing Pressure to Avoid Stress	73
Scaling Exercise	76
Using the Principles of Cognitive Behavioural Theory	77
Conclusion	79

5 Engaging in Reflective Practice — 81
Clare Stone

Introduction	81
Key Points	82
Significance for Social Work Practice	83
Using in Practice	84
Reflection on Practice	87
Reflective Questions	90
The Reflective Cycle	92
Reflecting on a Learning Activity	92
Using Art to Reflect	93

Developing a Reflective Learning Action Plan	94
Conclusion	95

6 Advanced Critical Reflection Through Narrative (Re)Construction — 96
Clare Stone

Introduction	96
Key Points	97
Significance for Social Work Practice	97
Using in Practice	98
Tools	102
Conclusion	104

7 Supervision for Transformative Learning and the Development of Practice — 105
Pam Snowball

Introduction	105
Key Points	106
Significance for Social Work Practice	106
Using in Practice	107
The Supervisory Relationship	107
Supervision History	108
Supervisee's Rights and Responsibilities	109
The Supervision Contract	111
The Supervision Agenda	112
Reflective Supervision	114
Role Clarity	114
Emotional Intelligence	115
Observation and Assessment of the Worker's Capabilities	115
Appropriate Partnership and Power	116
Peer and Group Supervision	120
Conclusion	121

8 Coaching for Social Workers — 122
Bobby Chatterjee

Introduction	122
Key Points	123
Significance for Social Work Practice	124
Using in Practice	124
The ACORN Model	129
Emotional Vocabulary	130
Visualisation	132
Conclusion	134

9 Learning About and Learning From Service Users — 135
Clare Stone and David R. Catherall

Introduction	135
Key Points	137
Significance for Social Work Practice	138
Using in Practice	140
Tools	142
Induction to a Building or Service	143
A Day in the Life of…	143
The Community We Live In	145
Who are the Users of our Service?	146
Feedback	147
Conclusion	152

10 Developing Digital Competence for Practice — 154
Joanne Westwood and Amanda M. L. Taylor

Introduction	154
Social Media	154
Social Networking Sites	155
Digital Competence and Digital Literacy	156
Web2.0	156
Virtual Learning Environment	156
Key Points	156
Significance for Social Work Practice	157
Using in Practice	160
Case Studies	163
Resources	165
Conclusion	166

11 Book Groups and Fiction: A 'Novel' Approach to Teaching and Learning — 168
Amanda M. L. Taylor

Introduction	168
Key Points	170
Significance for Social Work Practice	171
Using in Practice	172
Tuning into the Work and the Social Work Process	175
Dialectical Journaling: Pedagogy and Practice	176
Recommended Reading List	178
Conclusion	179

12	**Social Work Narratives: My Learning Journey** *Sue Gardner, Heidi Harbin, Amanda Murphy and Susan Woods*	**181**
	Sue Gardner: Newly Qualified Social Worker	181
	Heidi Harbin: Senior Social Worker and Best Interest Assessor	184
	Amanda Murphy: Independent Social Worker and Approved Mental Health Professional, and Former Principal Social Worker	186
	Susan Woods: Retired Social Worker and Independent Reviewing Officer Specialising in Child Protection Plans and Care Plans for Looked-After Children	189

Conclusion — **192**
Clare Stone and Fiona Harbin

Blibliography — 195
Index — 209

LIST OF ILLUSTRATIONS

Figures

i.1	The practitioner tree	3
i.2	The developing practitioner tree	7
1.1	How UCLan works in partnership with employers to support NQSWs	22
5.1	Reflective cycle	92
8.1	ACORN model	129
10.1	Mapping technology usage	161

Templates

1.1	Reflective practice cycle	16
1.2	Self-assessment audit tool	18
2.1	Learning plan using the principles of constructive alignment	34
2.2	Reflecting on the practice of others	37
2.3	Card sort activity: Service users and carers want their social worker to be/to have	39
2.4	Engaging with a text	41
2.5	Learning and development record	43
2.6	Learning agreement/learning contract for learning in the workplace	44
2.7	Employability development profile	45
2.8	Learning plan for career development/advancement	48
3.1	Developing insights into emotional competence: step one	58
3.2	Developing insights into emotional competence: step two	58
3.3	Developing insights into emotional competence: step three	59
3.4	Tune into emotions. Awareness of inter and intra aspects of emotional competence	59
3.5	Self-efficacy questionnaire	61

4.1	Bolstering confidence	72
4.2	Building resilience	76
4.3	Developing resilience through cognitive change	79
5.1	Reflection on practice	88
5.2	Reflective questions	90
5.3	Reflecting on a learning activity	93
5.4	Reflective learning action plan	95
6.1	Advanced critical reflection through narrative (re)construction	103
7.1	Supervision history	109
7.2	Supervisee's rights and responsibilities	110
7.3	Supervision contract	111
7.4	Supervision agenda	113
7.5	Emotional intelligence within the supervision relationship	115
7.6	Partnership and power in supervision	116
7.7	Reflective questions for supervision	118
7.8	Addressing anxieties in supervision	119
8.1	Difficult situations and powerful questions	125
8.2	ACORN coaching	130
8.3	Emotional vocabulary	132
8.4	Goal visualisation	134
9.1	Induction to a building or service	143
9.2	A day in the life of a service user or carer	144
9.3	The community we live in	145
9.4	Standard service user or carer feedback template	149
9.5	Easy read feedback template	151
11.1	Tuning into social work process	176
11.2	Dialectical journaling	177

CONTRIBUTORS

David R. Catherall
Following a variety of careers, which includes the police force, international marketing and project management in local government, David is now retired. For six years David was a carer for a man who had a severe and enduring mental health condition. He stopped being a carer due to his own ill health and is now enjoying involvement with Community Engagement and Service User Support (COMENSUS) at UCLan. He is a long-standing member of this centre and contributes to the education of social workers, nurses and medics.

Bobby Chatterjee
Bobby Chatterjee has over 15 years' experience as a business coach, and is currently a management consultant specialising in talent and leadership development. She works with a wide variety of sectors, facilitating groups of up to 400 participants. She has coached individuals at all levels up to main board and trained others to coach to an internationally accredited standard. She has supported and coached student social workers during their early career and is passionate about the difference that coaching can make to both confidence and competence.

Fiona Harbin
Fiona is a senior lecturer in the School of Social work, Care and Community at UCLan. Prior to joining the university, Fiona worked for over 20 years as a social worker with children and families. Her most recent social work post was as a manager of a Think Family team, which was a pilot project funded to work holistically with children and their families. Fiona has a particular interest in parental substance misuse and safeguarding children and has researched and written in this area. She has recently been involved in research focusing on parents' perceptions of the Common Assessment Framework. Fiona is committed to research informed practice and

is the module leader for a range of continuing professional development modules for qualified social workers.

Pam Snowball
Pam started her career as a social worker in child protection, and has worked for several local authorities and in both further and higher education institutions. She is currently a Workforce Development Manager in Bolton Council where she delivers in-service training for social workers across Children and Adults Services. Pam is also an associate lecturer at UCLan. Pam has a particular interest in supervision and assessment and in bringing together theory and practice to support social workers in the development of their knowledge and skills.

Dr Clare Stone
Clare is a registered social worker who worked within statutory adult services before moving into academia as a senior lecturer at the University of Central Lancashire. She has experience in managing the practice learning team and is module leader for a range of postgraduate post-qualifying modules. Her current areas of responsibility include working within the Centre for Continuing Professional Development, coordinating Making Research Count and leading an employability module for final year initial training students. Clare's doctoral thesis considers competence for social work practice.

Amanda M. L. Taylor
Amanda Taylor is a senior lecturer in the School of Social work, Care and Community at the University of Central Lancashire. Amanda's previous employment was as a social worker in the fields of psychiatry, mental health and deafness and as a specialist social worker for children with varying degrees of deafness, all set within the Northern Ireland Integrative Health and Social Care Structure. Amanda has been nominated and won a number of teaching and learning awards for her teaching innovations and is well known for the development of a national social work book group. She is particularly interested in creative teaching methodologies in social work education and continues in her endeavours to innovate in this area.

Dr Joanne Westwood
Joanne Westwood is a senior lecturer in the School of Applied Social Science at the University of Stirling where she is the programme

director for the social work qualifying programmes. Joanne is qualified in social work and has practised with children and families in England. Joanne has researched and published work on integrating social media in social work education and she is working with colleagues from across the UK on projects utilising the benefits of digital technology for both social work education and practice.

Chapter 12 Narrative Contributors

Sue Gardner
Sue Gardner qualified as a social worker in 2013. She is currently working as an Adoption Social Worker with responsibility for the assessment and support of adopters, family finding and providing support to the family throughout the adoption placement. She has a particular interest in Children Looked After and finding ways to practise that improve the lives of children in the care system.

Heidi Harbin
Heidi Harbin qualified as a social worker in 1998. She is currently working as a Best Interest Assessor for Bolton Council. She has responsibility for carrying out best interest assessments under the deprivation of liberty safeguards. She has a particular interest in safeguarding adults.

Amanda Murphy
Amanda Murphy qualified as a social worker in 1999. She is currently working as an Independent Social Worker and has a particular interest in mental health; she is also a qualified Approved Mental Health Professional and Best Interest Assessor.

Susan Woods
Susan Woods qualified as a social worker in 1984 after working as a primary school teacher. She has enjoyed more than 30 years of working predominantly with children and their families as a social worker and manager. Before retiring in 2015 she worked as an independent reviewing officer.

ACKNOWLEDGEMENTS

Clare and Fiona would like to thank David, Pam, Bobbie, Joanne and Amanda for contributing their chapters to this book, and the social work practitioners, Sue, Heidi, Amanda and Susan for sharing their learning journeys.

A special thank you to those who have given permission for us to draw upon their work. In particular we would like to thank Jacquie Morrison who has given her support for Pam Snowball to 'use and develop' Tony Morrison's work. Thank you to Jonathan Parker for not only allowing Clare to draw upon his self-efficacy questionnaire but also making suggestions as to the phrasing within the guidance.

The illustration of the tree and the images within the service user and carer feedback template have all been designed by James Lawless jamielawless13@gmail.com.

Introduction

Clare Stone and Fiona Harbin

Initial social work qualifying courses provide the basic foundations for social work knowledge, skills and values, and successful completion of these courses enables individuals to apply for registration as social workers. Qualifying courses therefore provide social workers with a good initial educational experience before beginning their journey into social work practice. However, such social work programmes do not equip individuals with everything they will ever need to know as social workers, nor do they train for specific social work roles. Social work practitioners need to keep abreast of the latest developments in knowledge and policy, consolidate the values that underpin practice and continually develop the requisite skills. For example the laws that govern social work practice change and the new knowledge generated through research shapes practice guidance. Therefore keeping up to date is an ongoing task throughout one's career.

There is a wealth of material already available, which focuses on the development of specific knowledge, skills and values for social work, therefore we do not replicate those within this book. Instead, our book focuses upon the individual as a lifelong reflective motivated learner. Jack and Donnellan (2010) suggest that to over-focus on what the practitioner needs to know and be able to do can result in failure 'to properly recognise the person within the developing professional' (Jack & Donnellan, 2010:305). Similarly Bates and colleagues (2010) claim that ongoing advancement of one's capability for social work 'is aligned to the concept of professional development as "being" rather than just "knowing"' (Bates et al., 2010:155). This relates to 'the person of the practitioner' or one's use of 'self' because being is 'an integral component of the learning and growing process in social work education' (Larrison, 2010:7). With this in mind we ask readers to attend to the individuality of professional development – of being a social worker, of the transforming self – because recognising the personal self within professional development is part of becoming a capable and safe practitioner.

Here we use the term 'self' to cover three domains:

> 'Self' as in accepting that one **needs** to learn, relearn and develop.

> 'Self' as in **how** one learns. What works well for one person may be a less useful activity for another individual.

> 'Self' as in **aspects** of self that need consolidating, refining, challenging and developing.

This book is about learning and developing the professional self. The first part of self is **accepting that one needs to learn**, relearn and develop, and this requires an understanding of the difference between initial education and post-qualifying development.

Within the United Kingdom there has been, and still is, a great deal of public criticism levelled at social workers and social work training. This can be traced back to the inquiry into the death of Maria Colwell in 1973, which resulted in the introduction of a social work award to provide a national standard. However, criticism of the profession continued and here we include a very small selection of the concerns about the capability of social workers. The inquiry into the death of Jasmine Beckford in 1984 concluded: 'qualifying training in social work adjudged unfit for purpose' (Slater, 2007:750). The high-profile death of Peter Connelly (Baby P) became 'a catalyst for public and government criticism of social work practice, management and training' (Bellinger, 2010:2451). The Social Work Task Force (SWTF) claimed that 'social work in England too often falls short of ... basic conditions for success' and included training as an area of weakness (SWTF, 2009:6). They went on to say that some students 'are being passed who are not competent or suitable for front-line social work' (SWTF, 2009:20). Munro (2011) agreed with those before her that 'not all newly qualified social workers are emerging from degree courses with the necessary knowledge, skills and expertise' (Munro, 2011:97). More recently Narey (2014) expressed his view that 'the preparation of students for children's social work is too often inadequate' (Narey, 2014:3).

Whether in the UK or in any other country, rather than lambast the social work profession the sector must accept that initial education is just that: it is initial and therefore it is the start. It is what

Eraut (1998) describes as the 'qualification–competence gap' to identify the difference between 'competence on a relevant degree course' and professional capability (Eraut, 1998:130, 135). The Oxford English Dictionary definition of 'initial' states:

> Of or pertaining to a beginning; existing at, or constituting, the beginning of some action or process; existing at the outset; primary; sometimes = elementary, rudimentary. (OED, 2015)

A tree is a helpful way to conceptualise the difference between passing a university programme and gaining competence in practice (see Figure i.1). The roots represent the initial education and the postgraduate training are the parts of the tree above ground level.

Figure i.1 The practitioner tree

The university helps to establish the roots, the firm foundation upon which the individual will continue to grow and develop once in employment. Therefore, those within the profession must accept there is a need to acknowledge and take responsibility for ongoing learning and development beyond initial social work programmes. Individuals do not leave university as 'finished products' but need to continue to grow and develop. They will have new experiences, face new challenges and have an increase in responsibility as they begin their social work career.

Research suggests that confidence increases during initial training (Carpenter, Shardlow, Patsios & Wood, 2015) to the point where newly qualified social workers (NQSWs) 'started their first jobs with optimism and confidence' (Jack & Donnellan, 2010:305). However 'around three months into employment, NQSWs would recognise the complexity of the social work in practice and consider that they had been less competent than they had thought at the start' (Carpenter et al., 2015:171). This resonates with the experiences of the authors who recognise a difference between the highly structured practice learning placement and the practice environment where the individual has increased responsibility and is expected to know and be able to do a great deal, often with less support and structure to their learning experience. Graduates often experience a dip in confidence as they realise there is a great deal more to learn and skills still to develop. Carpenter et al. (2015) suggest that although confidence develops and accumulates it is wrong to view 'qualifying education as the end product' (Carpenter et al., 2015:171). In their academic roles, both authors support NQSWs and have the great pleasure of working with motivated, engaged adult learners who are keen to learn, and reflection is the underpinning of their practice. The importance of ongoing development is heard through their reflective writing and a number have expressed the shock of experiencing a difference between the supportive final placement and the realities of practising as a social worker. The acceleration of responsibility from student to practitioner was even experienced by a NQSW who had two practice learning placements within local authority teams and another who had worked as a social work assistant for a number of years. One used the word 'terror' and many others used emotive language to describe feeling overwhelmed by the pace and nature of the work. Although it is concerning to hear the experiences of these graduates, it does echo published research into the experiences of newly qualified workers.

The individual does not leave the university knowing everything there is to know about their chosen profession, but has in place the foundation upon which self-development for professional practice can be built.

Because 'there are elements of professional development and learning that cannot be covered within the formal, generic degree programme', individuals will need to learn new things relevant to their specialist role (Bates et al., 2010:154). In addition, social work is never static and practitioners need to keep abreast of legislation changes and the advancement of knowledge. Therefore, accepting that one needs to learn, relearn and develop throughout their career is essential for maintaining safe and effective social work practice.

Returning to the notion of 'self' within continuing professional development we now explore **the 'how' of learning**. As the practitioner settles into their new setting they will begin to learn the norms, cultures, specific knowledge and processes related to that specific role and will continue to develop as practitioners. Structured programmes, such as the Assessed and Supported Year in Employment (ASYE) in England and Wales, are designed to support NQSWs through their first year in practice and do appear to have value in supporting the transition from university. Research findings suggest that the ASYE scheme encourages individuals to reflect and to develop essential skills (Kelleher, 2015); it also helps to develop professional confidence, prompts reflective practice, offers structured support and facilitates opportunity to discuss training and developmental needs (Berry-Lound & Rowe, 2013). Therefore, these types of structured programmes are a helpful way of supporting individuals to develop skills, knowledge and professional confidence during the transition from university to employment. A similar supportive framework would be advantageous throughout an individual's entire career. Although the employer of social workers has certain responsibilities (such as to offer comprehensive induction, supervision, support and teaching, for example) individuals need to take responsibility for their own learning and cannot expect employers to provide for their every learning need. Indeed the Health and Care Professions Council makes it clear that 'responsible employers will want to encourage the development of their staff' but it is the individual registrant's responsibility to meet the standards for continuing professional development (CPD) and they can 'remove registrants off [the] Register if they have not met' the standards for CPD (HCPC., 2012a:4).

The message is clear: it is the individual's responsibility to manage their own ongoing learning needs, but when it comes to doing this we advise that they explore and draw upon available support and resources. To further consider the how of learning, this book provides a basic overview to learning theory and offers tools and techniques that the reader may find helpful along their learning journey. Reflective learning is a central and prominent theme throughout this book because we value it as an essential methodology for workplace learning. We explain the need for individuals to reflect upon their experiences, to celebrate their strengths and identify areas to develop. Throughout the book a range of learning techniques is offered and the reader is guided towards identifying and developing supportive structures for aiding their learning journey.

Earlier in the chapter we introduced the idea that professional development needs to attend to the 'being' of the practitioner and transforming the self. We have already considered why one needs to learn and how one may learn, and now we consider **which aspects of self** need consolidating, refining, challenging and developing. Knowledge, skills and values, of course, need continuous updating and there are lots of texts readily available to support the development of these essential domains. In this book we do touch on the development of knowledge, skills and values but this is within the context of transforming and developing the professional self. When working with qualifying and post-qualifying learners, some individuals stand out because they have a personal quality/something about their approach and use of self that is intuitively recognised. One of the authors in her research found that practice educators (social work professionals who support and assess students on placement) differentiate between competence to pass a final placement and capability for social work practice in terms of that individual's approach to learning, resilience and emotional intelligence (Stone, 2014). An individual may do well enough to pass a final placement but it is the attributes within these three concepts that give practice educators confidence that the student will become a capable practitioner. Students who ask questions, are motivated to learn and are reflective were spoken about in positive terms. Capability for social work practice was also expressed in terms of emotional intelligence and resilience. Stone (2014) concluded that one's approach to learning, resilience and emotional intelligence was perceived by practice educators to be essential for effective and safe practice. These three domains all draw attention to the use of self within social work.

This book therefore has two chapters devoted to reflection and a chapter each concerning the development of emotional intelligence and resilience for social work practice. Although there is a growing body of literature about the need to have emotional intelligence and resilience, there is little practical guidance currently available about how they can be developed. We hope you find that these chapters (and of course all those within the book) offer practical and straightforward ways to develop the professional self.

We return to the illustration of the tree in Figure i.2 to pull together all of the points made so far.

The roots represent the generic initial training which creates the foundation upon which the individual will grow

The tree trunk, branches and leaves represent the individual's professional journey, post-qualifying, where they:
- continue to grow and develop
- learn specialist knowledge and skills
- consolidate values
- develop confidence and capabilities within their specialist area of practice.

Figure i.2 The developing practitioner tree

The breadth and depth of knowledge, skills and value introduced in qualifying courses provides the strong roots essential for healthy growth and development. The roots become the foundation that feeds the nutrition upward. The professional journey continues at the point of graduation, as the individual needs to consolidate and develop confidence, competence and capability through a range of learning activities. Their journey in practice takes them into new specialist areas and they will experience new ways of working. The individual needs to keep abreast of new knowledge, practice guidance and legislation. The professional self is continually shaped and reshaped. However, the tree does not need to stand alone but can draw upon a range of resources to sustain development and help survival during difficult times.

Despite the public discourse of a failing social work profession, and research findings that suggest more ought to be done to raise the calibre of social workers, we have seen individuals grow like our strong tree. We celebrate those individuals who grow and develop their professional self and we recognise the fantastic work that we have the great pleasure of witnessing on a daily basis. As academics, we visit social work and social care agencies to support students on placement, we are invited by social work employers to deliver bespoke training, and through our research and teaching, we engage with practitioners from all service types. These opportunities enable us to engage with remarkable individuals who do outstanding work, complex work, life-saving work and life-changing work. It is through learning and attending to their ongoing continued professional development that they are able to maintain effective and safe practice.

How You May Use This Book

This book has two main audiences: the learners, and the supporters of those who are learning. The learner may be a student, a newly qualified social worker or any other practitioner who wishes to attend to their own professional learning and development. We also anticipate that educators will find value in the text and will be able to use or adapt the exercises for working with individual learners or groups of learners, whether in the classroom or in workplace settings, with students or post-qualified staff. Although we speak to the social work profession in this book, others within health, education or wider social care may find value in the content. The exercises and templates throughout the book frequently use the term 'you' to encourage the learner to focus upon themselves and their own position, understandings and professional development.

Although we would love people to read every word, this book is set out in such a way that we hope it enables individuals to dip in and out as desired; to go straight to the bits of interest and places we have suggested where inclusions link to other sections. Each chapter follows a similar but not identical format, which usually comprises a brief theoretical introduction to the topic and outlines key points. Each chapter relates the theoretical to the practice of capacity building for social work practice. The aim is that readers will celebrate their strengths and learn things about themselves that will impact upon and improve practice. Therefore, we offer a range of tools, techniques and templates that are useful in developing self within professional practice. These tools can be employed in the classroom, during practice learning placement or in supervision, or individuals may try the techniques alone, in groups or with a mentor.

How the Book is Structured

This book is structured to focus upon the transformative self for safe and effective practice. The first chapter considers the transition from student to practitioner and considers how the social work learning journey can be managed. The challenges faced by NQSWs entering the workplace are explored and the chapter concludes that social workers need to continue to develop throughout their careers.

From Chapter 2 onwards, attention is given to what aspects of self can be developed and how they can be developed. Chapter 2 itself provides a basic theoretical underpinning to learning, with the aim of encouraging individuals to become a motivated engaged lifelong learner. Experiential learning coupled with reflective practice are situated as important and provide the platform upon which the rest of the chapters develop. The importance of the professional self as having and developing emotional intelligence and resilience are addressed in Chapters 3 and 4 respectively.

The following eight chapters focus upon the 'how of learning'. Reflective practice is explored in Chapter 5 and Chapter 6 introduces an advanced form of reflection through analysing narratives. Chapter 7 makes the case that supervision and particularly reflective supervision is essential for learning and professional development. The following four chapters present a range of approaches to learning and include coaching, learning from service users, digital learning and engaging with fiction for learning.

We are delighted that practitioners are contributing to our book in the form of reflections upon their learning journeys. Each social worker has taken a different journey since qualifying, but a common theme is the value they place on continued professional development and learning, to both keep abreast of changes and to cope with the complex and emotionally demanding nature of social work.

The concluding chapter, of course, rounds off the book by pulling together the main themes. We hope you enjoy reading this book and find it of value in transformative learning in and for social work practice.

1
The Transition from Student to Practitioner: Managing the Social Work Learning Journey

Fiona Harbin

Introduction

This chapter explores the challenges faced by newly qualified social workers (NQSW) entering into the workplace as qualified practitioners. Consideration is given to the role of higher education institutions and their necessary focus on education for the profession rather than training individuals for specific social care jobs. The chapter explores the pathway between the two settings and how this can be successfully negotiated, not only through a supportive working environment but also through the use of critically reflective tools during the transition period and beyond. Social work takes place in diverse settings and individuals need to learn in practice – building on, and supplementing their formal teaching foundations.

Social work, by its very nature, places the practitioner in a challenging and often emotionally demanding position. Social workers are required 'to negotiate the sometimes uncomfortable tensions between Government diktat, employer responsibilities and the social justice needs of those who use services' (Bates et al., 2010: 115). This negotiation is very often undertaken in the context of work carried out with individuals and families who are facing crises and trauma and may or may not be accommodating of the social work role. Social workers, by the very nature of their work, are most likely to meet and work with the people who suffer most as a result of poverty and inequalities in society. At a time of rising inequality this presents as most noticeable.

Social work placement experiences in the field will begin to equip the student with the skills necessary to manage the social work task. However, the protected environment cannot fully replicate the real-life experiences of a qualified social worker. NQSWs often report being overwhelmed by the levels of responsibility they feel when taking on a caseload of their own and having to manage this with often far less formal supervision than was experienced as a student. Urdang (2010) recognised that students 'generally do not anticipate the psychological stress and the changes they will undergo in developing a professional self' (2010:523). Many NQSWs clearly indicate that they feel overwhelmed by this context. Almost half of workers report an unmanageable workload (Liquid Personnel & Munro, 2015) and many feel ill-equipped and fearful of taking the perceived daunting step into professional practice. In their study of newly qualified staff Bates et al. (2010) found that while most were satisfied with, and spoke positively about their social work degree education, there were areas which were regularly identified as lacking. Interestingly many of these areas related to the development of resilience and skills required to manage the social work role rather than the actual social work tasks.

It is apparent that there is a commonality between research findings, most specifically the reporting of being given a high workload, but not having the skills needed to manage this in practice. As workload increases, social workers have a tendency to internalise their own perceived skills deficit in its management (Bates, 2011). This self-blaming response can be particularly challenging for workers early in their career as the focus is on gaps in their own management skills, when in fact their high workload is a systemic issue that can only be fully addressed through changes within the system and the provision of more resources.

The NQSW must be well equipped to manage the development of their professional self in the face of the demands of social work practice, in a social work world of increasing workloads and increasing complexity, and in the context of higher and more explicit academic and professional expectations.

The gap between qualification and practice cannot be underestimated and newly qualified social workers require support and guidance in developing strategies that will allow them to rise to these challenges and bridge this gap. Social work qualifying education provides the fundamental knowledge, skills and values required for social work practice in the context of the contemporary social work setting. Graduates must be prepared with, not only these attributes, but also with self-motivation as a core condition to negotiate the challenges and develop their own seamless learning experience.

Key Points

- Social work learning is a continuous process.
- The step from student social worker to qualified social work practitioner is a large one.
- Even the best social work education cannot fully prepare the newly qualified social worker for the challenges that lie ahead.
- The new social worker must take responsibility to develop their own skills, rooted in the skills and knowledge gleaned through academic study and on placement.
- The first years in social work practice are when the social worker is continually building upon their knowledge and skills, along with their resilience to manage the emotional and academic demands of the job.
- Self-management and an emerging developmental style are the first of many steps through career progression.
- Professional development is the responsibility of the individual worker, coupled with the support of a confident and knowledgeable supervisor/manager.
- Critically reflective tools can support social workers through this transition.

Significance for Social Work Practice

Over a period of time there has been an increase in the regulation of social work education and an increasing requirement of social work practitioners to manage and develop their own professional development, following qualification.

The professionalisation of social work is well documented (Bogg and Challis, 2013). The Central Council for the Education and Training of Social Workers (CCETSW) was set up in 1971 and since this time the social work role, and the training that social workers receive to gain a social work qualification and to ensure good professional practice, has become more prescriptive. 'Two years after the death of Maria Colwell in 1973 the CQSW [Certificate of Qualification in Social Work] was introduced to provide a national standard for professional training' (Stone, 2014:18). The death of Jasmine Beckford in 1984 refocused public attention on the failings of social workers and the sort of training they receive. The inquiry into Beckford's death concluded 'qualifying training in social work adjudged unfit for purpose' and this led to the CQSW being replaced by the Diploma in Social Work (DipSW) (Slater, 2007:750). Following ongoing concerns in relation to the preparedness for practice, all new social work graduates had to obtain a degree-level qualification as a minimum requirement to practise in the profession (General Social Care Council, 2002).

Since 2003, the requirement of continuing professional development as the key to competent practice has been explicitly laid out by professional and regulatory bodies. For those entering the professional practice sphere from academia the most noticeable and pertinent of these have been the NQSW status and the subsequent Assessed and Supported Year in Employment (ASYE) as detailed in the Professional Capabilities Framework (The College of Social Work, 2013). The NQSW status and the ASYE are not mandatory, but their attraction and popularity, as a means of both assessing and supporting the development of competence and capability, lies in their recognition of the challenges faced by early career social workers managing the transition from student to qualified practitioner and in their intention to guide the social worker through this. Many social workers have been supported by their employers to complete reflective portfolios as part of these schemes (Liquid Personnel & Munro, 2015).

Since the professionalisation process began there has been a significant shift in the perception of the individual social worker. There has been a move from the expectation that social workers are purely self-motivated, well-intentioned and caring individuals to the requirement that social workers must be all of these in addition to being well-educated, competent and regulated professional practitioners. This has inevitably placed a significant demand on the social work practitioner. Social workers have always faced challenges when entering into the professional sphere, and while this must be acknowledged, it is in fact the contemporary picture that can be viewed as far more problematic. Social workers must now not only contemplate managing the political context of the social care services, the higher demand for services (Liquid Personnel & Munro, 2015) and their increasingly demanding and regulated role requirements (Brown et al., 2009), but also the proficiency standards of their regulatory body.

Building on the opportunities and support available in the work environment, the individual social worker must embrace the principles of professional development and put into place a model for their own learning, which can support them not only through their transition from student to practitioner but also throughout their career. Reflective practice can support this transition and enable the individual to manage the emotional pressures, maintain professional responsibilities and protect against the possibility of burnout. Reflective practice can be seen as a 'basic cornerstone for the development of the professional self' (Urdang 2010: 524).

While there are frameworks that offer support and structure for the management and assessment of capability and competence, these are only truly effective if the individual practitioner takes on the responsibility for their own development.

What follows are examples of how reflective tools and practice approaches can support this transition process.

Using in Practice

This reflective tool, for use with a university tutor or social work supervisor, enables the progressing student and NQSW to consider the various stages of their professional development. The tool can then be used to identify the very different challenges that each stage will offer. As with many life changes, once the decision to change has been made, the maintaining and management of this can present the most significant challenges and for the new social worker this can be the optimal time to develop not only a style of practice but the internal and external resources needed to manage the emotional and capability requirements of the profession. Working towards resilience at this stage can greatly enhance a developing social work career.

This tool is rooted in the stages of cyclical change (Prochaska and Diclemente 1982) in recognition of the potential for change that the career path, followed by many social workers, may present along the way. Through personal choice, or enforced redeployment and restructuring, the model can be used to plan for, and manage, inevitable change. Starting at the pre-contemplation stage the social worker can use the reflective tool to identify key barriers and enablers to their progression by following the arrows around the cycle. There are neither time limits nor constraints to this process and the cycle may represent the changes made in one day or over the course of a few years. To achieve the best outcome, the social worker may complete the cycle several times. This cycle can be used as the basis of a dialogue or as a template for written completion.

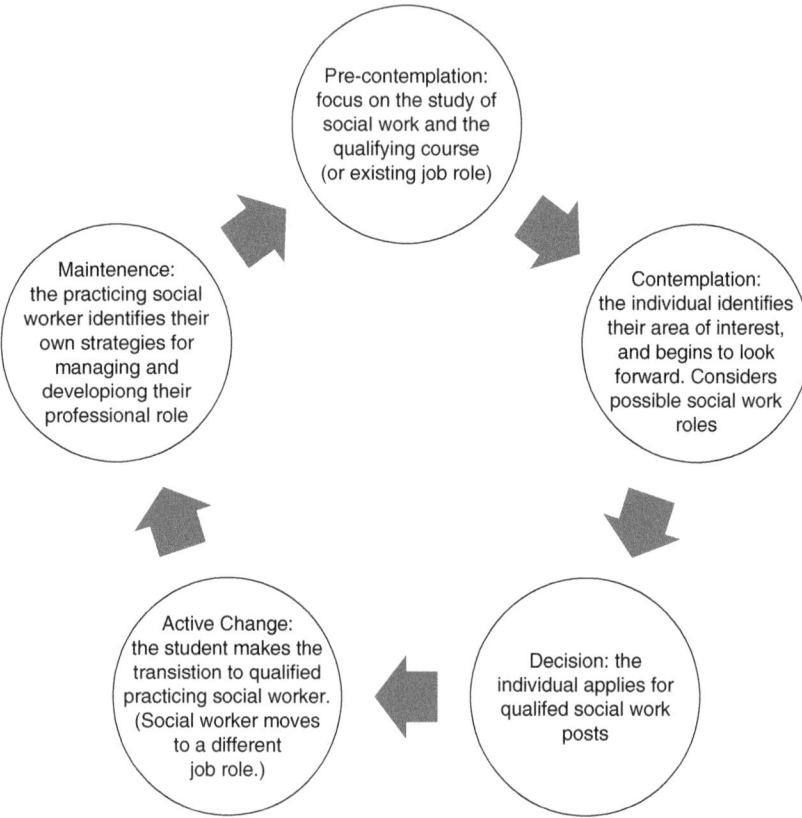

Template 1.1 Reflective practice cycle

Case Study 1.1: **Using the Reflective Practice Cycle**

Sarah has just started her first job in an adult safeguarding team. She had started her social work education with a plan to work with children but having had an inspirational placement experience with older people she refocused her interest on safeguarding adults. By using the change tool with her university tutor at the **contemplation** stage, she was able to identify the knowledge and experience that she would require for work in this field and to enhance her personal statement on her application for work. To supplement her academic knowledge and placement experience, Sarah then chose to work part time in a residential care setting and was able to further develop her skills of communication and general practical understanding of adult social care.

Reflecting on her situation at the **decision** stage, with an increased knowledge base encompassing both formal and practice knowledge, Sarah had nurtured the confidence and the keenness to apply for qualified social work posts in adult services. Her application form drew on her broadened knowledge base and enthusiasm to develop this further.

The transition from student to qualified worker, as considered earlier in the chapter, can be a difficult one. Using the tool to reflect on this, at the **active change** stage, Sarah was able to discuss with her supervisor what the most significant challenges would be for her. She based this on the areas that she would like to develop further, her previous practice experience and her formal knowledge. She recognised the progressive nature of social work development. She also identified her own skills and knowledge base and how these would benefit her practice and provide the basis from which to learn. She formulated a developmental plan with her supervisor based on these factors. A learning plan for career development/advancement can be found in Chapter 2.

Within the first year of practice, like many others, Sarah was developing her own emotional resilience for practice and broadening her knowledge base and confidence. In discussions with her supervisor and through the use of critically reflective practice Sarah entered the **maintenance** stage of the cycle. She recognised that, for her, managing the emotional impact of hostility from service users and carers and the demands of prioritising a busy workload were the greatest challenges. To ensure continued good practice Sarah used her supervision to consider her own personal strategies for addressing these issues, while at the same time recognising the limitations she may have as an individual to elicit change. Sarah's plan included working with her supervisor to ensure that she regularly finished work on time and did not work at home in the evenings; timely dialogue with her supervisor if she was struggling to meet deadlines; and utilising her theoretical knowledge base to inform her practice and explain hostile behaviour, thus depersonalising this and moving away from self-blame.

Sarah is still in her first social work post, but there is the possibility of a reorganisation within the department. Sarah may wish to use the tool to help her manage any potential changes that she may face. The concepts explored in this case study are further considered in the chapters on Emotional Intelligence (Chapter 3), Resilience (Chapter 4) and Supervision (Chapter 7).

Self-Assessment Audit Tool: Skills and Knowledge

Munro (2002) uses a circle model to illustrate the coming together of essential parts to form a coherent whole. Dalzell and Sawyer (2007) used this model to explore the skills and expertise required for undertaking assessments in social work. This can be developed further as a self-assessment audit tool to enable NQSWs and other practitioners to audit their own knowledge and skills. Rather than a cyclical approach, this is a visual pie chart that details many of the key elements informing successful social work practice. Through reflection on the topics identified qualifying and new social workers can scale their own confidence knowledge and experience. This can then be recreated as a personal chart with the segments sized to correspond to individual circumstances (remembering this should always add up to the whole).

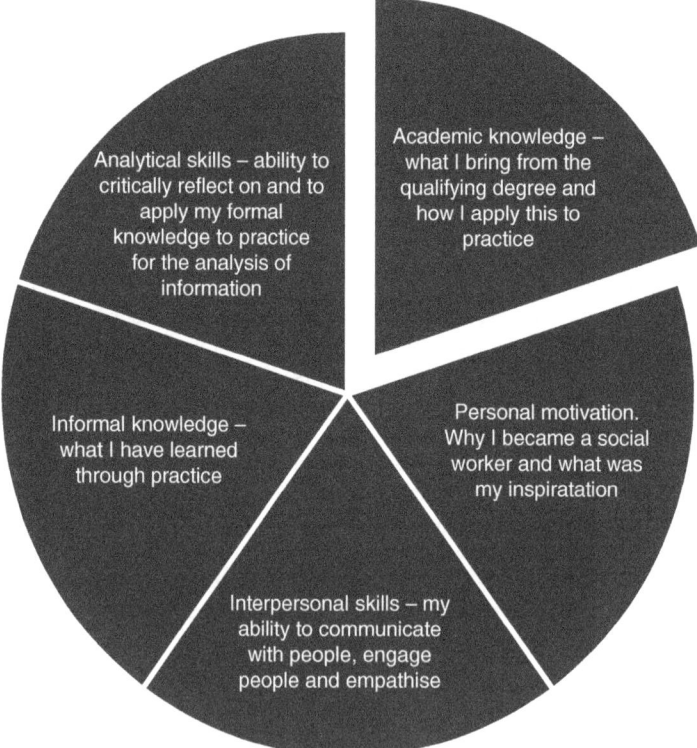

Template 1.2 Self-assessment audit tool

THE TRANSITION FROM STUDENT TO PRACTITIONER

The model has its roots in the core elements of knowledge first identified by Aristotle as intellectual virtue:

Episteme (theory)

Techne (practice)

Phronesis (value and context, application of knowledge)

(Fook 2012)

This model utilises the concept of **informal knowledge** as informal theory, which values the social worker's own ideas, developed through their own experience. It encompasses the concepts of 'practice wisdom' (Doel and Shardlow, 1993) and common practice knowledge. The model recognises the importance of **academic, theoretical knowledge**. This is knowledge identified as academic knowledge that can be named and traced to a specific source such as a writer or thinker (Mclean and Harrison, 2015).

The pie chart segment related to interpersonal skills promotes reflection on communication, self-awareness and emotional intelligence. Key to social work practice, emotional intelligence will inform how a practitioner is able to implement a theoretical intervention or approach. The model identifies the significance of values and motivation to practice.

To undertake this Self-Assessment Audit, draw a circle and then divide it up into five segments. The size of the segments is determined by your perceived confidence in relation to each of the named areas. Using this tool with a colleague, a supervisor or as a self-reflective exercise, the practitioner can plan how to develop their skills in any area that is lacking and address any overreliance on any one part of the chart. While there is no correct chart a well-rounded practitioner should be aiming for similarity in segment size.

Case Study 1.2: **Using the Self-Assessment Audit Tool**

Alam had worked in a child protection team for six months. His supervisor introduced him to the self-assessment audit tool and asked him to complete this in relation to a particularly complex child abuse investigation he had undertaken with a colleague. Alam spent some time completing the pie chart and took this in to his supervision to discuss. Alam immediately noticed that the sections on informal knowledge and analytical skills were significantly smaller than the other sections.

Through reflective discussion Alam was able to identify that this was the first investigation into child sexual abuse that he had undertaken and he had very little experience in this area. He had allowed his colleague to lead and he had added very little to the dialogue during this piece of work. While confident in his academic knowledge of the law and procedure in this area, Alam recognised that he was overly reliant on his own values and views in the analysis of the information gathered. Alam recognised that he had not used theoretical evidence to inform the analysis as he had struggled to apply his formal knowledge to practice.

Alam used the reflective discussion to identify a plan to rebalance his own skills and knowledge diagram. He identified an experienced colleague who he could shadow during a child sexual abuse investigation, he arranged to spend a day with the specialist police team and he identified two journal articles on analysis in child protection assessment which he would read and share with his team. Alam planned to revisit his skills diagram in two months' time.

Case Study 1.3: **Partnership Working: Employers and Academic Institutions**

Close working partnerships between universities and local employers can support the transition of social workers into the professional workplace.

Building on the partnership model, the University of Central Lancashire (UCLan) has an established history of working with local statutory, voluntary and independent organisations to support NQSWs through their first year in practice. The partnership has developed an academic, postgraduate module which complements a reflective portfolio completed by candidates and their assessors in the workplace. The module has evolved as changes in professional requirements and expectations have been implemented, allowing it to accommodate the transition from one professional body to another.

This module is designed for NQSWs during their Assessed and Supported Year in Employment to enable them to consolidate their social work knowledge, skills and values in their specialist area of practice. The module enables candidates to critically reflect on and review their development to facilitate enhanced performance and service delivery. Practitioners are supported to map their career progression against current professional benchmarks for continuing professional development.

The NQSW is enrolled on the module at UCLan as they commence their first year in practice. The university hosts two workshops, which focus on the engagement in critical thinking and writing. These workshops are normally attended within the first three months of employment and then in the second half of the year. As students of UCLan, the candidates are offered comprehensive learning materials, access to a named personal tutor, and the full range of university services which include, for example, the library, welfare service and sports facilities. These workshops track individual progress and provide interactive exercises to facilitate peer learning. This enables the social workers to maintain their links with an academic institution and receive support during the first stage of their post-qualifying journey.

Candidates work on a comprehensive portfolio with their employer that charts their development over the 12 months. Within this portfolio they produce a more detailed reflective academic piece addressing their developing specialist knowledge. This provides an opportunity for candidates to develop in-depth thinking about an area of their practice. It is this element of the portfolio that is marked with a percentage grade by academic staff and enables the practitioner to obtain postgraduate credits for their year in practice.

The candidate submits their portfolio on completion of the 12-month period to a panel made up of local managers and university staff. There are multiple layers of moderation at play in this partnership approach, without the process becoming difficult or overly bureaucratic. The employer has a role in ensuring consistency across their newly qualified staff and the panel is made up of representatives from more than one employer, as well as university staff members. The academic pieces conform to usual academic standards, including internal Higher Educational Institution moderation, and the external examiners ensure moderation at the national level.

The partnership originally used National ASYE documentation but this has evolved to meet local need. The portfolio offers the core templates that are required for candidates to meet the basic professional requirements and the academic module learning outcomes but employers can also add in their own documents and templates. The content ensures that the NQSW is responsible for the construction of the portfolio and supports them in taking responsibility for their own learning.

This model is being used with great effect to support and offer moderation across a range of organisations, including small voluntary and independent organisations both locally and nationally. By undertaking university modules such as this, the learner receives validation for their professional development, which is recognised both nationally and internationally. As the module is worth one-third of a Postgraduate Certificate social workers are encouraged to regard this as the start of their post-qualifying learning journey to complement other learning activities within the workplace.

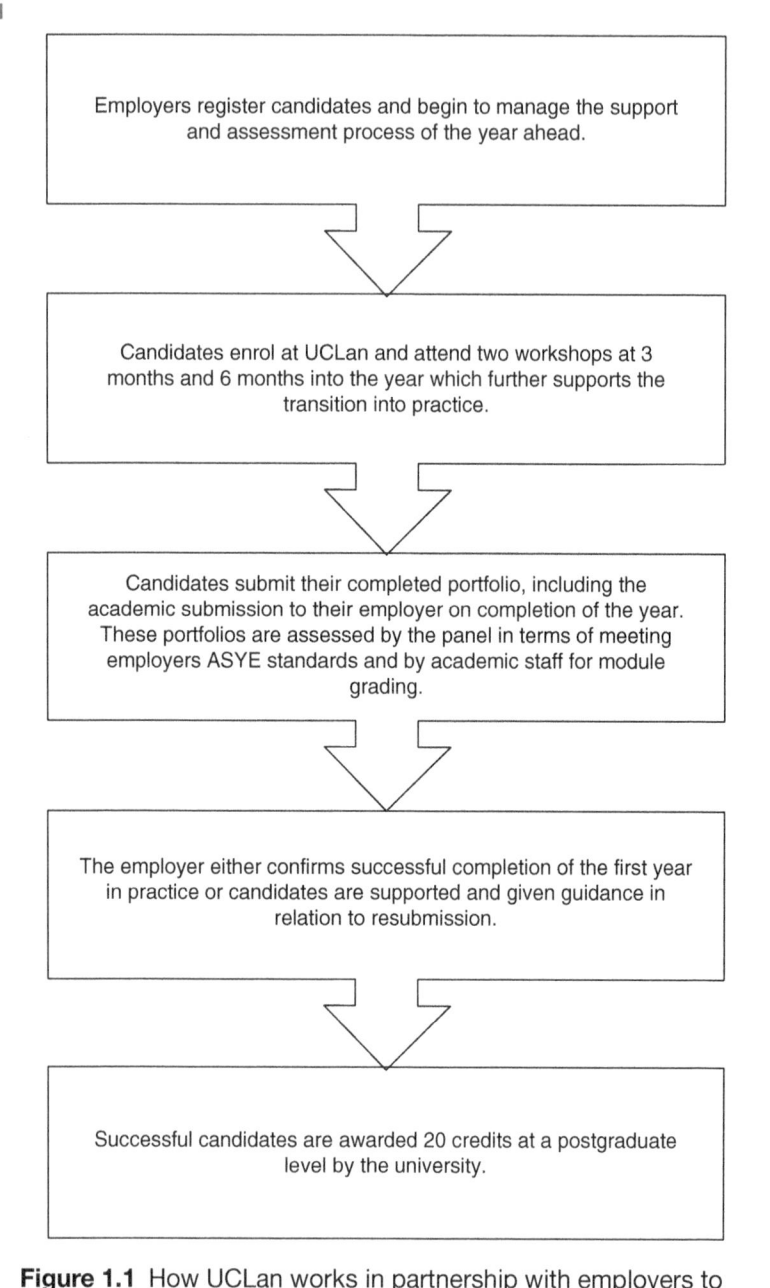

Figure 1.1 How UCLan works in partnership with employers to support NQSWs

Conclusion

The social work journey begins, for most practitioners, years before qualifying. It is not a profession that people enter into without a considerable amount of deliberation and thought. Although motivation to provide a good service in the chosen field of practice is high, the social worker will, however, face many challenges and changes throughout their career. As Thompson and Thompson (2015: 384) indicate, 'Social work is not a static entity.' The ability to manage the challenges and changes they have experienced is integral, not only to good social work practice, but to ensuring personal resilience to survive the emotional and physical demands of the work. By recognising the inevitability of transitions the social worker can work towards ensuring that they are equipped with the relevant skills to manage these changes.

The step from student social worker to qualified social work practitioner is a large one and even the best social work education cannot fully prepare the newly qualified worker for the challenges that lie ahead. The new social worker must take responsibility in developing their own skills rooted in the skills and knowledge gleaned from academic study and on placement. It is often in these first years of social work practice that the social worker begins to build, not only their knowledge and skills, but also their resilience to manage the emotional and academic demands of the work.

The development of learning and self-management styles during the first years in practice are the first of many steps through career progression. Social workers soon realise that, although there will be learning opportunities within their workplace, holistic and meaningful professional development is the responsibility of the individual worker, ideally with the support of a confident and knowledgeable supervisor/manager.

Critically reflective tools and collaborative learning structures, such as those offered within this chapter, can support social workers through the transitions they will face. These can support workers to embed a reflective and reflexive style in their practice but also in their understanding of their own learning and development. Serious consideration of continuing professional development and the management of changes in work practice is no longer just an option for the professionally qualified social worker, but is in fact an essential part of their professional responsibility and can significantly enhance their practice and ultimately the outcomes for service users.

2

Embedding the Principles of Adult Learning

Clare Stone

Introduction

Initial training provides the foundations of generic social work knowledge, an exploration of values for professional practice and the opportunity to develop the skills required to begin a first job. However, graduating social workers will not have a complete toolkit to steer them through the complexities of social work practice. Social work is recognised to be a fluid and ever changing profession and an individual needs to continually learn and relearn (Dickens, 2011). The political, legislative, financial, cultural and social contexts that underpin and shape practice are always changing and practitioners need to keep abreast of developing research and knowledge.

In addition to developing knowledge, social workers also need to bolster their skills and reflect on the values that consolidate their practice. Ongoing learning and professional development is essential throughout a social worker's career in order to work towards safe and competent practice. Social workers need to be lifelong learners because 'the professional self is continually reassessed and evolves' (Larrison & Korr, 2013:201). The graduate has the basics to begin practice but ongoing development is required to keep up to date, revaluate professionalism and maintain high quality interventions.

Within that context this chapter explores the nature of adult learning and how it can be utilised to promote continuous professional development in social workers and for social work practice. In line with professional expectations, practitioners are required to evidence their learning and development, and also consider the impact this has on their practice and particularly the outcomes for service users. The chapter offers guidance to support social workers through their career-long learning journey from qualifying courses to career advancement.

Key Points

Social workers need to engage in learning throughout their professional career to ensure safe and effective practice and to meet the regulatory body requirements of continued professional development. To be an effective adult learner:

- social workers need to be motivated, autonomous, reflective life-long learners;
- practitioners need to take responsibility for their learning and can be supported by peers, educators and managers; and
- social workers can engage with a range of traditional and more contemporary learning theories to understand and structure their learning and professional development.

Significance for Social Work Practice

In this section the terms 'andragogy' and 'transformative learning' are considered in relation to the continuing professional developmental needs of social workers. 'Andragogy' is a term used to differentiate adult learning from pedagogy, which relates to how children learn. Although Malcolm Knowles did not create the word 'andragogy', his work made the term very popular and his principles of andragogy still hold credibility and relevance today in adult education and in social work practice education (Gitterman, 2004; Walker, Crawford & Parker, 2008; Williams & Rutter, 2010). Knowles suggests that, as individuals mature, they become less dependent and more self-directing, have life experiences which can be drawn upon, focus on roles and tasks, and wish to apply learning more immediately. When these principles are put into practice, adults begin to take more responsibility for their learning; recognise their prior experience; are ready and orientated to learning; and have the motivation to learn (Knowles, 1984; Knowles, Holton & Swanson, 1998). Similarly Gibbs (1988) suggests that adults learn best when they have choice, set their own goals, have independence, have autonomy, build upon their reservoir of experiences, reflect, can apply the learning principles to practice, have learning activities which are active, focus on principles and learn from solving practice problems, and need to do all of this in a climate of openness and trust (Gibbs, 1988). The principles of Knowles and Gibbs are evident throughout this book and are the underpinning principles that have led to the design of the various tools and exercises offered.

However, the tools and exercises offered within this book are not enough to ensure that learning occurs because the principles of adult learning equally apply to the learner as to the teaching elements. Learning is not a one-way process from teacher/educator to learner, as it requires the adult learner to take responsibility for their learning by setting goals and engaging in reflective practice. The learner must consider and seek out supportive safe relationships and environments in which they can explore change for professional development. Filling in a template or following the instructions in an exercise will not necessarily lead to learning because the learner is required to be motivated to learn, willing to reflect upon their experiences and to work to amend their practice as a result of new knowledge and insights gained. It is important to recognise that in addition to the tools offered in this book, practitioners are encouraged to consider the learning potential within everyday life. When watching the news, reading an article or having an interaction with another person, take time to consider what can be learnt. Learning can be stimulated from naturally arising problems in social work practice and day-to-day life, not just from attending formal training or completing a set exercise.

Taking the adult learning principles into consideration the aim of this book is to support social workers to develop knowledge and skills and also work towards transformatory change. Although it has been around for many years, transformative learning theory 'is experiencing ever-increasing interest' (Taylor & Laros, 2014:135). In reply to the question, 'what are we trying to transform?' Illeris (2014a) suggests that when we talk of transformative learning, identity is perhaps the most useful concept (Illeris, 2014a). He favours identity because identity combines 'individuality and sociality' or put more simply, has psychosocial dimensions (Illeris, 2014b:577). Rather than conceptualising identity as being fixed in our formative years and set for the rest of our lives, we in fact continue to develop and change both internally and in the public facing aspects of identity.

Illeris suggests that individuals have three layers beginning with a core identity which includes biographical self-identity; second, a personality layer which influences the way we relate to others; and third, an outer preference layer which is enacted in the things we do, routines we practise, what we say and how situations make us feel (Illeris, 2014a). These three layers of identity have relevance to social work as identity impacts upon our thinking, how we approach situations, our relationships and work practices. In social work education and training we may learn new knowledge and skills but professional development is also about transforming the self and how we identify as a competent capable practitioner. The chapters within this book engage with transformative learning theory and the principles of andragogy as we ask the reader to think about personal development and the use of self which ultimately focuses attention onto the psychosocial – your identity as a social worker.

Transformative learning theory and andragogy encompass consideration of the individual experience, critical reflection, engaging in dialogue with the self and others, variety in teaching approaches, consideration of the context and relationships that foster learning (Taylor & Laros, 2014). It is through these principles that we can acquire skills and knowledge, and they also afford the opportunity to consider one's psychosocial identity: the core biographical self, how we interact and manage relationships and our performance in practice.

The principles within andragogy and those of transformative learning recognise the responsibility of both the learner and the facilitators of learning. However, to be motivated to learn 'the learning must be of considered subjective significance' to the individual (Illeris, 2002:153).

> In adulthood, when a relatively stable identity has been developed, motivation becomes a quite central issue in relation to possibilities of changes in the identity. The type and strength of the motivation involved is crucial: Adults do not transform elements of their identity if they do not have serious reasons for doing so. These reasons may be internal, external, or both, but analytically, the important thing is that transformations imply strong motivation and cannot be expected to occur without such motivation. (Illeris 2014a:159)

Biggs and Tang (2007) agree that motivation to learn comes from the expectancy that the subject is worth learning, has value and there is a chance of succeeding (Biggs & Tang, 2007). The learner therefore needs to have a voice in what is being learnt so they have an invested value and recognise the importance of the task. A learning contract or learning plan can be most useful here to negotiate and agree what is to be learnt, how it is to be learnt, the timeframe involved and the arrangements for support. Taking ownership of the learning package situates responsibility with the learner and maintains their active involvement and motivation to achieve. The templates provided later in this chapter are based upon the principles advocated here.

The transformative learning promoted in this book is not easy and requires real commitment. This commitment extends beyond ticking boxes and learning just enough to achieve a pass grade at initial training or during the probation and assessment of newly qualified social workers. Biggs and Tang (2007) claim that surface learners use 'low cognitive-levels' of activity to get the task out of the way (Biggs & Tang, 2007:22). Surface learners do the bare minimum needed to get by but this is an unhelpful approach to social work practice and practitioners need to move to a position of deeper learning where they are engaging on a cognitive level, critically questioning, analysing and making creative links.

Instead of conceptualising deep and surface learning as fixed binary positions, it is more helpful to think of them as a continuum along which a learner can be supported to move. Therefore, rather than label an individual as either a deep or a surface learner they ought to be encouraged to embrace more of the andragogy principles to become actively involved and invest in their own professional development. Individuals may well become deeper learners when they recognise the value of what they are learning, can apply it to practice, build upon prior learning and take ownership of the learning experience. Rather than doing the bare minimum, those who have a role in negotiating the learning package are more likely to engage in learning at a deeper level.

Research conducted by Bogo et al. (2006) and Stone (2014) both identify that an individual's approach to learning (motivated, enthusiastic and self-directed) is a characteristic that differentiates the 'exemplary students' (Bogo et al., 2006:306; Stone, 2014). Those who approached social work experiences as learning opportunities (were motivated, reflective and took responsibility for learning) are considered more likely to become more capable social work practitioners post qualifying (Stone, 2014). Hodkinson et al. (2008) suggest those who embrace learning during initial training are more likely to do so once they enter social work practice:

> For if we see people becoming through learning in the learning culture of one situation, they do so again, if and when they move to another the learning culture of a different situation. The person who has become through learning as a student, arrives in a workplace and continues to learn and become, as a worker. (Hodkinson, Biesta & James, 2008:43)

Therefore, during initial training the student must be a reflective, motivated and engaged learner but the learning must not stop at the point of passing the course. A student cannot learn everything during social work programmes and will need to continue learning once in a qualified role (Dickens, 2011; Larrison & Korr, 2013). They also need to continue to develop skills and maintain professional values through learning.

Social work practice provides a rich opportunity for learning. Social workers can learn directly from their practice experiences but this may require some to develop

> an alternative epistemological view, one that enables them to see themselves as creators of 'personal knowledge', rather than as containers to be 'filled', and that allows them to develop personal learning techniques. (Gamache, 2002:277)

Gamache (2002) uses the term personal knowledge and reminds us that we are creators of knowledge. Social workers engaged in social work practice can develop knowledge through their experiences. This turns our attention to the 'dynamic process' of practice wisdom (Thompson & West, 2013:118). Thompson and West (2013) remind us that in practice we draw upon background knowledge, empirical knowledge, theoretical knowledge, procedural knowledge and self(meta) knowledge (Thompson & West, 2013). It is through these different knowledge domains that we begin to understand which intern informs our responses. Our practice wisdom is the process by which we make appropriate use of knowledge, relevant to the practice situation, while reflecting to ensure we are responsive and intuitive. We therefore reflect while in the experience and reflect later to further develop our practice wisdom:

> Wise professionals recognize not just their own knowledge and procedures in practice, they also recognize their own ignorance and the client's

expertise. Thus wisdom lies in intuitively recognizing when deficiencies present a need for further theoretical and procedural knowledge and when there is a need for deference to client or other knowledge. (Thompson & West, 2013:125)

The templates and exercises throughout this book aim to encourage the development of practice wisdom and transformative change. This is because the content within the book provides background, empirical and theoretical knowledge, and encourages the individual to seek out procedural knowledge and consider self-(meta-)knowledge. Individuals are encouraged to draw upon these knowledge domains appropriately and responsively, and are also asked to identify ongoing learning needs. This book encourages individuals to engage with the andragogy principles and become a deeper type of learner. Some of the activities within this book target specific development and others are more general learning. However, all require a disposition to learning: for the learner to be motivated, reflective and committed to lifelong learning in order that they develop practice knowledge and to transform the self.

Using in Practice

So far, consideration has been given to how adults learn best (the principles of andragogy) and how transformative learning theory draws our attention to transforming identity in addition to developing skills and learning new knowledge. Social workers need to be lifelong learners: social work changes constantly and so should the practitioner. The social worker must continually evaluate and develop the psychosocial dimensions which include consideration of the interplay between self, others and practice. To facilitate one's own learning or the learning of others, some understanding of learning theory and principles of learning is helpful. What follows is a very small selection of some learning theories to encourage consideration in relation to the how of learning: the epistemology. By no means is this a comprehensive list of all theories of how people learn or theories in relation to teaching techniques but it is a small selection of traditional and more contemporary theories which the reader may find of value or at least interesting.

Behaviour Modification

In the late 1890s the Russian physiologist Ivan Pavlov was measuring the secretion of saliva and noticed that his dogs would begin to salivate whenever he entered the room because they had learnt to associate his presence (stimuli) with food. He experimented and found that other stimuli could be paired with food to elicit a salivation response in dogs. For example, Pavlov sounded a bell before presenting the food and after doing this a few times the dog began to associate the bell with the food and they began to salivate on hearing the bell because they anticipated getting food. When a behaviour is elicited (learnt or modified) as a direct result of a stimulus it is called classical conditioning.

B. F. Skinner extended the work of Pavlov by introducing the law of effect through reinforcement. Skinner demonstrated that by reinforcing (also called rewarding) certain behaviour, that behaviour is more likely to be repeated. It is easy to think of examples from our own lived experience where we have seen behaviour repeated because of a reinforcer; think about how children will repeatedly make silly noises when they are rewarded by becoming the focus of attention. This is referred to as operant conditioning and the principles can be successfully used to teach new behaviours or modify existing behaviour.

Repeating a behaviour over and over helps improve performance and we can relate this to our own experiences, for example, in sport, baking or using a piece of equipment. The old saying that practice makes perfect is relevant here and Pritchard (2014) explains that practising behaviour develops neural pathways in the brain which result in faster and smoother responses and actions (Pritchard, 2014). However, behaviourism is not traditionally interested in what happens in the brain (the mental activity) because its focus is on the observable behaviour which comes about through conditioning: a reaction to a particular stimulus (Pritchard, 2014).

Social learning theory builds upon these same conditioning principles. The individual imitates the language, actions and behaviours and is duly rewarded by acceptance into the group or community. Consider how individuals behave in new settings and how quickly they imitate language, behaviour and customs to fit in with peers. Although the famous Bandura Bobo doll experiment showed that children learnt and could imitate aggressive behaviour through observational learning, they did not imitate and copy what they had seen if the child actor was chastised for hitting the Bobo doll. Unlike Skinner, Albert Bandura considered the cognitive aspects at play as individuals are able to explore the relationship between behaviour and its consequences. The relevance here to social work learning is that we do imitate and copy behaviour (for example, modelling which is addressed later in this chapter) and we also have automatic subconscious reactions (this is further explored in Chapter 3 in relation to emotional intelligence). However, as adult learners, the thought processes at play (cognitive engagement) have a much stronger role in behaviour, action and learning.

Cognition Within Learning

Cognition refers to what goes on in our brains and is therefore the mental process of learning. The work of Jean Piaget is well known and is a helpful way to understand the age related intellectual developmental stages in children. Children begin by seeing things only from their own position but develop to a point where they are able to take into account the perspectives and feelings of others. As individuals mentally mature they construct unique views of the world structured through their own lived experiences. We draw upon what we have experienced and what we have learnt to construct our own perspective and to help us understand the situations we are faced with. This construction is fluid and ever-changing because it is influenced by new information, new experiences and importantly is influenced by our interactions with others.

Cognitive behavioural therapy (CBT) uses these principles to help individuals explore why they behave in certain ways in certain situations and supports them to reconstruct alternative perspectives and different ways of responding to stimuli. Identifying a behaviour that is having undesirable outcomes or a behaviour that limits practice is the starting point. Through honest reflection the individual identifies what triggers this behaviour; what is the stimulus that makes them respond in this way? This process may take some time and talking through with a supportive and trusted other is advisable as they can use prompts and probe questions. The open-ended questioning technique used by the supporter may encourage the other to reflect upon things not previously thought about, revisit experiences, recount observations, explores anxieties previously kept hidden or other similar lived experiences. The aim is to make a link between antecedents/stimuli and why they may trigger particular behaviours and responses. The next learning step in CBT is to cognitively engage with this knowledge and be open to new ways of thinking so as to guide new ways of responding. Again the support of the trusted other is valuable to help reconstruct an alternative perspective.

Although CBT is a therapeutic technique the principles can be used within social work learning to help individuals explore things that limit learning and development. Students, for example, may find it useful to identify triggers that block their focus and lead to displacement activities. Newly qualified social workers can explore in supervision their emotional reaction and the supervisor can support them to practise alternative responses. In common with most of the content of this book, engaging with cognition to construct alternative behaviours requires honest reflection, a desire to learn and strong motivation to persist in professional development. In Chapter 4 the principles of CBT are drawn upon in relation to developing resilience for social work practice.

Constructive Alignment

'Constructive' in constructive alignment refers to the idea that the learner must construct meaning through relevant learning activities (Biggs & Tang, 2007). The alignment refers to ensuring there is a logical relationship between what needs to be learnt, how it will be learnt and how the learning will be reviewed (or assessed) (Biggs, 1996). To begin, start by asking what does the learner want/need to be able to do and what do they need to know. These may be outlined in the form of prescribed learning outcomes, competence statements or other such aims, which guide what needs to be learnt or achieved. The second stage is to decide the best way to go about obtaining this knowledge or skill. For example, it may be appropriate to read a policy document to obtain procedural knowledge but reading will not enable the development of specific skills. Skills development needs a more practical activity, which affords the opportunity to develop both confidence and competence. The activity of learning must be appropriate to what needs to be learnt and also of meaning to the learner. In relation to assessment it is important to consider the most appropriate method to test that the learning has occurred. For example, a written exam will not test the acquisition and enactment of skills and therefore the assessment has to be aligned to the aims of the learning. In addition to assessing at the end of the learning period (summative assessment) it may be appropriate to review progress during the period of learning to assess whether further guidance, learning opportunities or support is required (this is called formative assessment). Feedback can be obtained during the learning period to provide confidence and further direction as required.

Constructive alignment is widely used in education because teachers/lecturers/ facilitators are required to plan and audit learning. The principle of constructive alignment also adds value to learning in the workplace as it offers clarity and a constructed relationship of learning and development. Template 2.1 can be used to negotiate and document a learning plan which draws upon the principles of constructive alignment.

Template 2.1 Learning plan using the principles of constructive alignment

What needs to be learnt?	How will it be learnt?	How will I know it has been learnt?	What support will be offered?	Review date

Learning Taxonomy

Bloom (and educational psychologist colleagues) developed a classification of levels of intellectual engagement which during the 1990s was updated by Anderson (and cognitive psychologist colleagues) (Forehand, 2012). The intellectual levels are ordered into a hierarchy and referred to as a taxonomy. The first level of the learning taxonomy requires the learner to remember and then as they progress up through the hierarchy they are required to use different cognitive abilities to the point where they are able to undertake creativity in practice. The levels within the taxonomy are remembering, understanding, applying, analysing, evaluating and finally creating. If we apply this to social work practice there are some things that social workers need to remember and times when they need to recall information but they must also understand it. It is no good rote learning sections and subsections of legislation without understanding the application within the practice setting. The cognitive levels of analysis and evaluation resonate with what social workers are required to do in practice as they appraise, judge and defend their conclusions. At the top of the taxonomy is 'creating' and this is about constructing alternatives, formulating new opportunities and developing appropriate interventions. Creating person-centred care packages and risk management strategies requires this level of cognitive engagement.

The language within the taxonomy can be employed in the constructive alignment activity above so, rather than write that the learner needs to know A, B and C it may be more appropriate to include phrases such as 'critically evaluate the principle of A in relation to B'. Those supporting the learning can use the taxonomy to help the learner consider the cognitive levels at play and also to assess their ability. In supervision, for example, select a social work theory, model, policy guidance or piece of legislation and work through the taxonomies. What can the learner remember about X, what does X mean, how does X apply to the situation of the service user, how useful and how limiting is X to the service user's situation, are there alternative ways of using or presenting X that can support the service user, and what else can be drawn upon to assist him or her? This moves the thinking to a position of critical engagement with a practice methodology or policy, thereby cognitively considering impact upon practice and the people we work with.

Using the taxonomy as building blocks of cognitive activity actively involves the learner and focuses learning which can have immediate and direct impact on their practice. Rather than learning a skill or obtaining knowledge that may be relevant at a later point in time, the learning can be immediately applied to a practice situation. Taxonomies of learning also link to Knowles' principles of andragogy (as previously explored) because it accepts that adults are not empty vessels but they already have knowledge and experiences that can be built upon and developed to achieve creative, thoughtful social work practice.

Learning Styles

Individuals are often asked in learning environments to complete a learning style inventory or questionnaire to identify what type of learner they are (some prefer the phrase cognitive style). There are many different types of inventories and 'instruments' available which learners can easily access in books or online (Cassidy, 2010:420). The outcome of the learning style assessment usually categorises the individual as a particular type of learner and may offer suggestions as to how best to facilitate learning for that person.

If individuals do complete one of the various learning style inventories, they ought to engage with the issued guidance and suggestions of how to use the outcomes in a meaningful way. Take time to consider how this knowledge can bolster learning rather than see the completion of the exercise as an end in itself. It is my experience that many enjoy the activity of completing the inventory yet very few engage in it as a tool for facilitating learning. By this I mean they do not engage with the suggestions of how to advance their own learning. I have experience of learners blaming educators for their lack of learning because they did not teach in a way that matched their learning style. Individuals may have a propensity towards a particular way of learning or thinking but to cope in social work they need to be able to translate information and cognitively manipulate it, regardless of the mode of communication. Service users will present information to practitioners in many different forms and the worker needs to be able to handle that appropriately: they cannot say my preferred style is auditory therefore please do not email me as I need you to verbally communicate all information. It is unreasonable to expect the teacher or learning environment to change as a result of an individual's particular preferred way to learn but there is advantage in opening dialogue with the learning facilitator. For example, in supervision share the outcome of the learning style inventory and discuss what this may mean to the learner and educator and how together you can capitalise on learning.

Riener and Willingham (2010) claims 'there is no credible evidence that learning styles exist' but conclude that individuals 'may have preferences in how to learn' (Riener & Willingham, 2010:33 & 35). Cotton (1995) suggests that learning style inventories is more of an indication of personality rather than learning style and she has experience of people using their learning style 'as an excuse for not getting on well at school' (Cotton, 1995:120). The message therefore is to complete a learning questionnaire if you wish but actively take responsibility to maximise learning. Like Cotton, I conclude that adults can draw upon a range of styles and select the style most relevant to the 'particular learning situation' but social workers need to be able to accept information in a range of mediums and also have the ability to present information in different formats (Cotton, 1995:120).

Modelling

Modelling is an effective way to learn skills for social work practice and therefore the learner needs to identify a good role model (Barretti, 2007; Mumm, 2006). Chambers (2012) claims that the 'vast majority of literature exploring the concept of role models does so from a positive perspective' (Chambers, 2012:47). This is because the learner can see the enactment of knowledge, skills and values within practice that they can aspire to emulate. Social work learners need 'direct experience of observing good professional practice and positive role models in order to facilitate their reflective learning and professional socialisation' (Wilson, 2013:168).

Rather than just shadowing a colleague or watching their day-to-day practice, it is important to reflect on what has been observed and Template 2.2 offers questions to stimulate this reflective process. Think back to the principles of social learning theory and cognitive engagement to make decisions about the value of what has been observed. A learner needs to ask questions such as: What aspects of the other person's practice work well? Which are the best bits that I wish to incorporate into my own practitioner style? and What values are evident in their work with service users and colleagues? Template 2.2 provides questions to reflect upon your observations, with a view to developing your own practice:

Template 2.2 Reflecting on the practice of others

Reflecting on the practice of others	
Who is a good role model?	
Why are they a good role model?	
How do they make me feel when I see them in practice with service users?	
What is it about their practice that makes me feel like this?	
How do they make me feel when I see them working alongside colleagues and other professionals?	

(Continued)

Template 2.2 (*Continued*)

What is it about their practice that makes me feel like this?	
What words or phrases do they use that are particularly useful?	
What aspects of non-verbal communication were particularly effective?	
What else do I value and recognise about their practitioner style?	
What is my plan to develop my own practice as a result of reflecting on the practice of others?	
What will be the value of observing/co-working with/shadowing this person again?	
How will I maintain a role modelling relationship with this person?	

Card Sort

A card sort is a useful learning exercise as it requires activity, thinking and engagement with others. Individual cards are produced which can include statements, pictures, symbols or individual words and the aim is to rank the cards 'into a continuum of significance' (Jahrami, Marnoch, & Gray, 2009:178). The continuum of significance can be one long line with the most important at the top and the least important at the bottom. Or it may be more appropriate to sort the cards into columns and the headings could be: strongly agree, agree, neither agree nor disagree, disagree and the final column would be strongly disagree.

Alternatively each card can be considered and the learners select only the top five and bottom five statements. Regardless of the way the cards are sorted it is important to pay attention to the thinking behind why the cards have been ranked in that particular way because the card sort can be a learning activity which aims 'to draw out a subjective opinion or view' (Ellingsen, Størksen & Stephens, 2010:400). The sorting exercise can be a catalyst for discussion and is therefore a useful exercise to do in groups or in pairs (Jahrami et al., 2009). The opportunity to hear another person's views and opinions can trigger deeper personal insight and open up the possibility of considering alternative ways of thinking. I have used card sort exercises a number of times and find them to be an active and engaging learning medium as participants quickly begin debating where the cards ought to be placed, listen to the opinions of others and negotiate a compromise of arranging the cards.

After sorting the cards, I ask learners to pay particular attention to those cards at the extremes of the hierarchy or those cards within the strongly agree and strongly disagree columns. I also ask:

- Does this ordering provide you with new insight?
- Is there a refocusing of priorities?
- Is a change to your practice required?

Template 2.3 provides the statements for a card sort exercise, designed to focus attention onto professional values and professional practice but, like all of the activities in this book, learners and educators are encouraged to edit and amend as appropriate. To begin with, write statements that are directly relevant to the service and setting, or change the theme completely and make it directly relevant to the topic of learning. After writing the statements, decide which may be the best way to begin sorting the cards and provide clear instructions. Think about creating a safe and supportive environment to encourage discussion and remember that there may not be a right or wrong way to sort the cards. If a good discussion happens and reflective learning is taking place it really does not matter if the cards remain unsorted because they have been a means to stimulate learning. Learners can do a card sort learning activity alone, in pairs with peers, in groups or within a supervision session.

Template 2.3 Card sort activity: Service users and carers want their social worker to be/to have

Fashionable clothes	Punctuality	Rule-following
Availability	Use words I understand	Spontaneity
Honesty	Courage	Attractive
Committed	Risk-taking	Loyalty
Vitality	Humility	Friendly

(Continued)

Template 2.3 (*Continued*)

Aware of services and resources	Knowledge about my situation	Come from same background as me
Power	Humour	Time to listen
Willing to bend rules	Integrity	Creativity
Caring	Cautiousness	Spirituality
Funny	Do what they say they will	Compassion
Live in the same community	Trustworthy	Awareness
Friendly	Kindness	Intelligence
Keep me informed of what is going on	Come in their own time to see me	Know lots of people
Respectful	Openness	Energetic

This card sort exercise asks the learner to think about what service users and carers require of social workers; what is most important to them? Therefore, the heading for the exercise is 'Services users and carers want their social worker to be/to have'. The cards need printing and cutting up into individual cards (think about the size of the card and the text). The instruction is to rank the statements into a continuum of significance, starting with the most important. I also like to provide a number of blank cards so learners can add their own statements.

Other Mediums for Supporting Learning

There are many opportunities to learn in and for social work practice and examples include:

- Reading policy documents, practice guidance, newspapers, literature, journal articles, and information on websites and textbooks.
- Watching television or videos. This can include the news, documentaries or video productions on line.
- Attending conferences, workshops and seminars.
- Peer group learning by way of action learning sets and learning circles.

The above list is not exhaustive but the common element is that the activity is a means to learning. Earlier, the point was made that one needs to actively engage in the experience and transformative learning requires motivation and a commitment to act upon the reflection. After watching a documentary you may find it helpful to discuss the content with others or write about your learning, using a template similar to Template 2.4 to help you focus on knowledge and practice.

Template 2.4 is designed to be used as a prompt to encourage engagement with the content of literature and can be completed alone or with a learning friend(s). The literature may be a section on theory relevant to social work, a research article, an article in a newspaper or any other writing whether it is academic, creative, fiction or factual. The questions in Template 2.4 encourage consideration of the links between new knowledge (or new ideas) and practice. However, as with all of the templates in this book it requires the learner to spend time thinking, making links to self-development, and there is a requirement to be motivated to want to learn and change practice as a result of new insights.

Template 2.4 Engaging with a text

Engaging with a text	
What are the main points the author is making in the writing?	
What is the author saying that is relevant to my area of work?	
What knowledge is new to me?	
How does this relate to my experiences?	
How can I use the findings/suggestions/recommendations in my work?	
What further learning do I need and how will I go about it?	

Reflective Supervision as Learning Methodology

A common theme throughout this book is the requirement to reflect in practice, reflect on practice and reflect for practice. Reflective practice has 'become an increasingly influential idea in social work education' (Wilson, 2013:154) and it is my experience that reflection is embedded within both the academic and practice components of initial and post-qualifying training. Another theme in this book is that learning can be done alone or as a social activity and supervision is an appropriate environment for learning. Done well, reflective supervision provides a supportive, collegial, safe and nurturing space in which reflection can take place.

There are many templates and exercises within this book that can be completed within the supervisory time and the supervisor can critically question, tease out tensions, play devil's advocate and facilitate deeper reflection. Alternatively the learner may do one of the exercises prior to the supervision and share their new insight with the supervisor. The supervisor may also be in a position to share additional materials such as feedback from colleagues or service users, or work-generated products, for example, records or reports to stimulate reflective learning. The supervisor and supervisee can work together to develop an action plan to address further learning and development needs. Chapter 7 further explores reflective supervision.

Recording Learning

Template 2.5 can be used to log learning activities but it also prompts consideration of the impact of learning. The learning activity can be anything which may include, but is not limited to, training within the workplace, a university module, supervision, experiential learning, shadowing, watching a documentary, completing an activity within this book, engaging in critical discussion with peers or any other experience upon which you cognitively and reflectively engage. The aim is to keep an ongoing continuous record which will be useful for professional reregistration and other purposes such as career advancement opportunities. Therefore, record the date and the location of where the activity took place, and give the activity a name. It is then important to concisely note what has been learnt and the impact this learning has on practice. Remember to note the benefit of this learning upon others such as peers, the agency and of course the users of the service. It may also be useful to think about how this learning and professional development meets professional body expectations, standards, learning outcomes, codes of practice and practice guidance. Template 2.5 can be amended to meet your individual learning needs and more columns and rows can be added.

Template 2.5 Learning and development record

	Learning and Development Record				
Date and place	Learning Activity (this can include training, supervision or any other learning activity)	What did you learn?	What is the impact on practice?	What is the benefit to service users, colleagues, agency or others?	Optional (e.g. link to professional standards / learning outcomes etc.)

Learning Agreement/Learning Contract for Learning in the Workplace

Template 2.6 uses the principles of constructive alignment to structure a learning agreement. It also draws upon the principles of andragogy because the emphasis is on the learner taking responsibility for the learning experience. Therefore, the questions in Template 2.6 are directly addressed to the learner by using the word 'you'. The template can be amended as required and additions may include, for example, learning outcomes and assessment criteria from formal study programmes and workplace learning requirements.

Template 2.6 Learning agreement/learning contract for learning in the workplace

Name of learner:	
What is to be learnt? *Here you need to clearly state what is to be achieved and one of the following prompts may help:* *During the period of learning I want to achieve …* *I want to be able to ….* *The learning outcomes/learning statements I have been given are …*	
Support	
What learning activities and tasks will you engage in to reach your learning objectives?	
Clearly identify your learning & support needs	
How will these needs be met?	
Reflective supervision will be provided by:	
Supervision sessions will be scheduled as follows:	
Expectations	
What expectations does the learner have of the supervisor/assessor/educator/agency?	
What expectations does the supervisor/assessor/educator/agency have of the learner?	
Review and Assessment	
When will my learning be reviewed? *Detail formative and summative assessment*	
What do I need to produce to evidence my learning? *Also provide details of set assessment tasks*	
Who will be involved in the review of my learning and how will feedback be given?	
Date and method of final assessment	
Agreement Summary	
Date of completion of agreement	
Learner signs to confirm they agree with the arrangements set out in this agreement	
Supervisor/assessor/educator signs to confirm they agree with the arrangements set out in this agreement	

Remember that the learning agreement/contract can be renegotiated and added to as many times as required.

Career Development and Career Advancement

Template 2.7 is an amended version of the CareerEDGE Employability Development Profile developed by Dacre Pool et al. (2014), which they designed to encourage students to think about employability in terms of strengths and areas for improvement. With their permission I have amended it slightly to make it directly relevant to those wishing to work within social care and social work.

Template 2.7 Employability development profile

My career aim is:
I would like to start my own business: Yes / No
Please respond to the following statements to help you identify possible areas for development. It is important that you try to answer as honestly and accurately as possible

1 Strongly disagree	2 Disagree	3 Slightly disagree	4 Neither agree nor disagree	5 Slightly agree	6 Agree	7 Strongly agree

Career Development Learning

1) I know what kinds of work would suit my personality — 1 2 3 4 5 6 7
2) Apart from money, I know what I want from my working life — 1 2 3 4 5 6 7
3) I know where to find out information about jobs that interest me — 1 2 3 4 5 6 7
4) I know what I want to do when I finish my course — 1 2 3 4 5 6 7
5) I know what is required for me to successfully secure the sort of work I want to do — 1 2 3 4 5 6 7

Experience Work/Life

6) I have a lot of placement and work-relevant experience — 1 2 3 4 5 6 7
7) I can explain the value of my experience to a potential employer — 1 2 3 4 5 6 7

(Continued)

Template 2.7 (*Continued*)

Degree Subject Knowledge

8)	I am satisfied with my academic performance so far	1	2	3	4	5	6	7
9)	My academic performance so far is in line with my career aspirations	1	2	3	4	5	6	7

Generic Skills

10)	I have good oral communication skills	1	2	3	4	5	6	7
11)	I am good at making presentations	1	2	3	4	5	6	7
12)	I am confident about my written communication skills for various audiences	1	2	3	4	5	6	7
13)	I work well in a team	1	2	3	4	5	6	7
14)	I work well independently	1	2	3	4	5	6	7
15)	I am good at solving problems	1	2	3	4	5	6	7
16)	I have good planning and organisation skills	1	2	3	4	5	6	7
17)	I manage my time effectively	1	2	3	4	5	6	7
18)	I am always open to new ideas	1	2	3	4	5	6	7
19)	I am prepared to accept responsibility for my decisions	1	2	3	4	5	6	7
20)	I have a good understanding of how the social care sector operates	1	2	3	4	5	6	7
21)	I am a confident user of information & communication technologies (ICT)	1	2	3	4	5	6	7
22)	I am satisfied with my level of numeracy	1	2	3	4	5	6	7
23)	I am good at coming up with new ideas	1	2	3	4	5	6	7
24)	I am able to adapt easily to new situations	1	2	3	4	5	6	7
25)	I can pay attention to detail when necessary	1	2	3	4	5	6	7

Emotional Intelligence

26)	I am good at working out what other people are feeling	1	2	3	4	5	6	7
27)	I am good at knowing how I am feeling at a given time	1	2	3	4	5	6	7
28)	I am able to manage my emotions effectively	1	2	3	4	5	6	7

	Questions	Range	My Score
Career Development Learning	1–5	5–35	
Experience Work/Life	6–7	2–14	

Degree Subject Knowledge	8–9	2–14
Generic Skills	10–25	16–112
Emotional Intelligence	26–28	3–21
Total Score	1–28	28–196 _____

Now take a look at the way you have scored the questionnaire. For the questions you have scored with a 6 or a 7, would you be able to demonstrate your abilities in these areas and give some good examples of these? Choose one of these highly rated areas and write how you would explain this to a potential employer.

Now take a look at the questions you have scored with a 1, 2, 3 or 4. What action could you take to help you increase these scores to a 6 or 7? Choose one of these items and write your action plan for this below.

When individuals have aspirations to change jobs or obtain promotion it is useful to consolidate learning and development and to draw up a career development plan. Template 2.8 begins by summarising learning and development to date and then looks ahead to the requirements of the new role to help identify appropriate areas for development.

Template 2.8 Learning plan for career development/advancement

Description of my current role (*include tasks and responsibilities*):		
The strengths and abilities I have to perform this role (*you may wish to consider knowledge, skills and values*):		
What I have achieved over the past year? (*summarise as you wish and you may consider including projects you have been involved in, performance, feedback and also review the targets you set last year*)		
My career goal is (*aspirations for the immediate and longer term*):		
To prepare for and to achieve I need to develop (*consider knowledge, skills, qualifications, training and experiences*):		
To develop	How I will develop this (remember to detail support requirements)	Time scale & review date
Additional notes:		

Acknowledging Challenges to Learning

If we accept that the principles of adult learning are to take responsibility for what and how we learn, be motivated, be reflective and embrace all experiences as potential learning opportunities, we can use this to recognise challenges to our learning.

Individuals need to ask themselves:

- What do I need and want to learn?
- How do I want to learn this?
- What support do I have?
- How can I create time to reflect on the learning?
- If I have limited motivation for learning, how can I make the task more enjoyable, linked to my previous experiences, recognise my strengths, recognise the value of the learning and focus on aspects I find most enjoyable?

It may also be appropriate to consider other internal factors impacting upon your learning, such as low confidence and not understanding what is expected of you. There may also be external influences that you need to consider, such as access to learning resources and other responsibilities dominating learning time.

Conclusion

In social work education and in practice there are many naturally arising situations from which we can learn. However, it takes more than participation in an activity to ensure transformative learning. As social workers, we need to take responsibility for our own learning, engage with learning opportunities, reflect upon our experiences and be motivated to change and develop our practice. We need to be dedicated to learn despite the setbacks and workload pressures – to carve out protected time and think about what is being learnt, the relevance to our developing professional self and then commit to a plan to enact the learning.

Individuals need to arrange opportunities that enable them to learn in a way that feels comfortable. They need to make links and networks, set up a peer learning group, find a mentor, observe colleagues, seek out suitable role models, contribute to setting the agenda for supervision to ensure there is reflective learning time, join e-learning groups or enrol in post qualifying training. Regardless of the activity it is essential that learners cognitively engage to recognise learning for practice and for the development of the professional self, and be committed and motivated to make that learning a transformative experience.

3
Fostering Emotional Intelligence Within Social Work Practice

Clare Stone

Introduction

Emotional intelligence is the ability to read our own and other people's emotions and to handle ourselves, and our interventions with others, appropriately (Goleman, 2004a, 2004b; Howe, 2008; Mayer et al., 2012). This includes understanding our own emotional responses to situations and being able to keep them in check to elicit a professional and appropriate response in a given situation. Emotional competence goes beyond putting people at ease and asking open-ended questions, as it requires a deeper level of understanding, compassion and engagement. Social work is a profession where the use of self is often the only resource available to draw upon and therefore 'tuning into' others is essential (Douglas, 2008:382). 'Competent practice is more than the application of techniques' as it requires 'integrated embodiment' through the use of self which fills the gap between knowing what to do and actually working with individuals in a skilled and effective way (Larrison, 2010:8, 6). Social workers need to build and maintain relationships with a range of people, not only with the people who use social work services, but also with their colleagues and the other professionals they work alongside. Working with individuals in crisis and responding appropriately in tense, uncertain situations requires highly tuned emotional intelligence. Emotional competence enables the practitioner to accurately read the situation and use both verbal and non-verbal responses appropriately.

Key Points

Emotional intelligence includes intrapersonal and interpersonal dimensions that enable an individual to understand and manage emotional well-being and work alongside others. Social workers need emotional competence to work with:

➢ Service users, their families and communities
➢ Individuals within the same team and organisation
➢ Other professionals and care providers

Emotional intelligence is not a fixed attribute but it can be developed through a range of techniques which include experiential learning and reflective practice.

Significance for Social Work Practice

As social work is a relational activity, the ability to work alongside others by understanding them and establishing effective communication is paramount. Within the professional encounter the practitioner requires emotional competence to identify and manage their own emotions and to recognise and respond to the emotions of others. 'Others' in this case may be work colleagues, managers, other professionals and of course the individuals and families who use social work and social care services. Emotional intelligence is essential for social work practice as the practitioner needs to relate 'especially well with service users' and colleagues in a wide array of contexts (Howe, 2008:180).

The intrapersonal aspect of emotional intelligence enables one to be self-aware by recognising how our thoughts impact on behaviours and feelings. Such insight enables one to control and 'rein in emotional impulses', regulate responses and thereby aid communication with others (Goleman, 2004a:xiii). Social workers work alongside individuals who are subject to very difficult circumstances and portraying that one is overwhelmed by hopelessness or too emotionally affected to be in a position to assist is unprofessional and counterproductive. Likewise the worker who fails to recognise their own increasing state of arousal may not respond in a safe manner and may inadvertently exacerbate a tense situation rather than defuse conflict.

The worker who understands and can manage their emotions in a positive way will feel more confident in their practice and be able to communicate more effectively, which will lead to them being a happier and safer practitioner. 'The emotionally intelligent person is often a pleasure to be around and leaves others feeling better … but does not mindlessly seek pleasure' (Salovey & Mayer, 1989:201). Conversely a social worker who experiences difficulty in managing their emotions will expend a great amount of emotional labour and find working as a social worker more difficult. 'Emotional labour is defined by the expenditure of intellectual, physical and emotional resources, time, effort and energy to identify/understand and fulfil one's own and other's emotional needs' (Megele, 2015:15). Higher levels of emotional intelligence are for this reason linked to resilience for social work practice, as those who are more in tune with emotions are less vulnerable to stress because they are happier and more competent within social work practice. Indeed, research by McFadden (2015) found that although social workers are at risk of burnout, their strong sense of accomplishment keeps them going (McFadden, 2015). (Chapter 4 provides a comprehensive exploration of resilience in social work.) This is because understanding one's own emotional state and being able to regulate responses has a positive impact on both the intrapersonal and interpersonal aspects of social work and therefore our relationships, success and competence in the role.

In addition to self-awareness, a person who is emotionally competent also has social awareness. Being able to accurately read other peoples' emotions will enable one to begin to develop empathetic understanding. Rather than just hearing the words and story of another, it is:

> about really tuning into their emotional worlds and gaining a deep understanding of how they perceive and experience their lives. Only by thinking about emotions and their impact on our lives can we truly communicate sensitively. (Ingram, 2015:64)

Mayer, Salovey & Caruso (2004) claim that people with higher emotional intelligence 'better perceive emotions, use them in thought, understand their meaning, and manage emotions better than others' (Mayer et al., 2004:210). This enables the social worker to begin to really understand meaning for that individual, gain clarity about their perspective and their unique position to inform appropriate responses.

An individual with emotional intelligence can say the right thing, know when to say nothing and appropriately offer comfort (Howe,

2008). Engelberg and Sjoberg (2005) use the term 'bi-directional exchange' to describe the interpersonal skills needed to interact in different settings (Engelberg & Sjoberg, 2005:295). Their research concluded that people with higher emotional intelligence are better able to adapt within social environments. The social environments and contexts in which social workers practice are varied and may include the need to contain anxiety, comfort those in despair or defuse tense situations. Emotional competence will also guide the analysis of information during assessment and help inform interventions. The worker who is socially aware and picks up on emotional cues is more effective in communication and thereby able to establish and maintain 'success in … relationships, both personal and professional' (Rosenthal, 2012:1).

Therefore, in summary, a practitioner who is emotionally competent 'understands that emotions affect behaviour, beliefs, perceptions, interpretations, thoughts and actions. The ability to adjust, modify and regulate our emotions as we relate with others is' important for social work practice (Howe, 2008:12).

> The emotionally intelligent practitioner may be more adequately equipped to develop and sustain the affective relationships that are at the heart of practice than practitioners who lack the attributes associated with emotional intelligence. (Ingram, 2013:988)

Using in Practice

Although the foundations for emotional intelligence are laid in childhood, emotional competence is not a fixed attribute and therefore can be developed into adulthood. Childhood is an important stage in the development of emotional intelligence and Howe (2008) makes theoretical links to attachment theory. He discusses how abused children may become adults in 'emotional pain' who 'avoid emotional intimacy' (Howe, 2008:62). This is because childhood is a crucial time for brain development and the individual learns how to respond in dangerous and arousing situations. Responses are honed through interactions with parents, siblings and peers (Goleman, 2004a). Therefore, if children do not have exposure to appropriate and supportive interactions they will not develop a repertoire of competent responses. As emotional intelligence is not fixed genetically it can be developed beyond childhood because it 'continues to develop as we go through life and learn from our experiences'

(Goleman, 2004b:7). Practice cultivates emotional competence so the more life experiences we have the more we can mature (Goleman, 2004b). The amygdala is the area of the brain that provides the automatic response to emotionally charged situations (Goleman, 2004a). Sensory information goes straight to the amygdala and bypasses the cortex, which results in a quick subconscious reaction. Such responses can be an adrenalin rush, dry mouth, flinching or making a verbal response such as shouting. This is because 'all emotions are, in essence, impulses to act' and derive from survival instincts (Goleman, 2004a:6). In childhood the brain makes neural connections and a stimulus produces an automatic spontaneous response (Goleman, 2004b). This type of stimulus response is akin to classic learning theory when Pavlov's dogs salivated to external stimuli.

However, we have two minds; an emotional mind that feels (amygdala) and a rational mind that thinks (neocortex) (Goleman, 2004a). Ideally these two parts of the mind work together and act to guide us during emotional and other arousing situations (Goleman, 2004a). When we say someone has responded without thinking, this is the amygdala emotional reaction rather than allowing the neocortex time for a more measured response. In social work it is essential that we have measured, rational and thoughtful responses rather than emotional and subconscious responses:

> Sadly it is not uncommon for social workers to encounter verbal abuse and aggression. Such situations are likely to generate a fight or flight response as a result of our bodies pumping adrenaline into our blood stream to prepare us for responding to the perceived threat. Thankfully, most aggression does not lead to actual violence, but our bodies do not know that and react accordingly. This can leave us feeling tense and agitated and therefore prone to reacting rashly and unwisely. Emotionally intelligent people use the thinking part of their brain and allow themselves time to have a considered response in emotional situations. We therefore have to make sure that we are able to train ourselves to respond to such situations as calmly as we can, difficult though that may be. (Thompson, 2013:69–70)

Thompson makes the point that although the social worker may intuitively recognise danger, a measured response is required rather than a subconscious automatic response such as raising the fist to defend or indeed to attack. Emotionally competent individuals do not respond in such primitive infantile ways because they have developed a range of responses through interactions with others during their formative years. Although the foundations for emotional intelligence are laid in childhood, our thought processes and repertoire of responses can be positive or negatively influenced. Therefore, those individuals who have less well-developed emotional competence and have a limited range of responses, which are appropriate for social work practice, can be supported to become less impulsive and trained to respond from the neocortex area of the brain. Goleman talks of the brain needing retooling to change habits of thought, feeling and behaviour (Goleman, 2004b). He goes on to suggest it requires effort and time because the neural connections make 'dominant pathways for nerve impulses' and these require retraining (Goleman, 2004b:243). Howe (2008) describes the brain as 'plastic' as it can restructure by making new and stronger connections as a result of new experiences (Howe, 2008:95). Saarni (2000) gives 'weight to learning and development' and suggests that it is important to have exposure to learning opportunities to develop emotional competence (Saarni, 2000:84). Therefore, with the right conditions individuals can learn and develop, to become more emotionally competent.

To develop emotional competence one needs to be motivated and to persist despite setbacks. Learning about oneself and learning how to appropriately respond in arousing situations takes time and therefore focusing on the development of emotional intelligence ought to commence at the outset of initial training and be revisited throughout one's career. Working in social work agencies, students and practitioners can 'use naturally arising opportunities' around them (Goleman, 2004b:252). The social work student usually receives one-to-one teaching and support from practice educators, and practitioners are supported by managers and supervisors and therefore learning can be tailored to the individual learner's needs. Experiential learning, feedback and engaging in reflective practice are key to emotional development. Learners need to have the opportunity to practise and receive supportive feedback to guide their learning. The learner must reflect on their experiences to recognise the things they have achieved and identify those areas that require development.

Although individuals can be supported to develop appropriate emotional responses this does take time, commitment and practice. Curriculum designers can identify specific opportunities in the university, early on in social work programmes, to begin developing emotional competence within learners. The final placement is an opportunity to fine-tune emotional competence in readiness for practice but it is not a long enough period of time to develop those students with low levels of emotional intelligence. It is therefore appropriate for universities to consider emotional intelligence at the admissions stage and throughout the initial training, and for employers to consider ongoing development post-qualification. The exercises in this chapter (and others within the book) use the principles of reflective practice to bring to the fore aspects of thinking and behaviour which impact upon practice. Through honest reflection, an opportunity is created to celebrate strengths and achievements and to identify those aspects that require improvement and development. Practitioners are encouraged to use the principles of observational learning, experiential learning and reflective practice to develop their own levels of emotional intelligence and emotional competence for social work practice.

Case Study 3.1

Jack is a newly qualified social worker who is working with families who have complex needs. Jack feels that the family has little confidence in him and he thinks they would prefer to have a more experienced social worker supporting them. Jack shared his concerns in supervision and his supervisor asked him to complete a self-efficacy questionnaire, which had been designed for practitioners working within children and family services. Jack worked his way through the questions, considering his confidence and ability to execute different aspects of practice. The discussion with his supervisor enabled Jack to reflect on his strengths and areas for development.

Jack explained that when he did not know the answer to a question or when the conversation was beginning to explore something he knew little about he would change the topic. His status as a newly qualified social worker and personal characteristics, such as being a single male who has no experience of having or raising children, made him feel as though he had little to offer families. He began to consider that his internal lack of confidence may have been impacting upon his communication with the service users. Jack's internal concern about 'being exposed as someone who did not know enough' was limiting the development of the relationship with service users. Jack's attention was drawn to intrapersonal aspects of emotional intelligence (the knowing of one's self) and how this was impacting within his practice. He was expending so much energy in not being exposed that he was not engaging in person-centred practice, not adequately present in the moment, not following the agenda of the service user and was not developing rapport.

The reflective supervision enabled Jack and his supervisor to celebrate the strengths within Jack's practice including his personal qualities and capabilities. It also provided the opportunity to identify further support and training to help develop Jack's emotional competence.

Case Study 3.2

Kara was five months into her first social work job within a community mental health team when she was asked to visit Petra, whose neighbours had telephoned to report their concerns about her deteriorated mental health. On visiting the property Kara found Petra to be unwell and it appeared that she been self-harming. In supervision she explained how she felt helpless and inadequate in her response when Petra had sworn at her, said she would kill herself and told Kara to go away. Kara and her supervisor used Template 3.4 entitled *Tune into emotions. Awareness of inter and intra aspects of emotional competence*. Kara was able to explore her feelings about Petra with her supervisor, that she felt sorry for Petra yet found it hard to understand why people self-harm. Kara began to question whether her responses may have projected sympathy rather than empathetic understanding and this led to Petra shouting at her. Exploring intra and interpersonal elements afforded Kara the opportunity to replay and re-evaluate her professional presentation and, with her supervisor, agreed to further relevant learning opportunities.

Knowing Oneself

An important aspect of emotional competence is to know oneself and Templates 3.1 through to 3.4 provide exercises designed to enable the individual to reflect in depth with the intention of helping them to have greater insight into their emotional competence. As Rosenthal says, 'it all starts with learning how to listen to your feelings. While it may not always be easy, developing the ability to tune in to your own emotions' is required to develop emotional intelligence (Rosenthal, 2012:1).

The first activity is to select a time in your life, a moment or a situation, where you felt that you did not fit in or felt uncomfortable with those around you. This can be from any aspect of your life, such as a private, social or family situation, your education or an experience at work. Then ask yourself the prompts and questions in Template 3.1. The aim of the exercises is not to apportion blame to yourself nor to others but to make a link between feelings and behaviour and to develop insight into your own emotional competence.

Template 3.1 Developing insights into emotional competence: step one

I felt uncomfortable or felt that I did not fit in or failed to relate well to others at/when:
I felt:
How did my feelings impact on my behaviour?
How might the other people have perceived/experienced me?
If I had a time machine and could make changes I would …
What have I learnt about myself?

Now, select a time in your life, a moment or a situation, where you felt very comfortable and able to relate well to others. As with the exercise above, this reflection can focus upon any area of your life. Again, the aim is to make a link between feelings and behaviour, and to develop insight into your own being.

Template 3.2 Developing insights into emotional competence: step two

I felt comfortable/fitted in/was able to relate well with others at/when:
I felt:
How did my feelings impact on my behaviour?
How might the other people have perceived/experienced me?
What have I learnt about myself?

It is important to reflect upon steps one and two and to consider what learning can be taken forward to other situations. Now complete the exercise in Template 3.3.

Template 3.3 Developing insights into emotional competence: step three

Summary of learning from both parts of the exercise
What learning can I take to other situations? How do I know myself a little better?

Template 3.4 is an alternative exercise to help you tune into your emotional competence through awareness of interpersonal and intrapersonal aspects.

Template 3.4 Tune into emotions. Awareness of inter and intra aspects of emotional competence

Think of a recent encounter with a service user or colleague and give a very brief outline from your exchange.	
What is your interpretation of their emotion (remember emotion can include many things including but not limited to them presenting as being happy, sad, anxious, excited).	
What non-verbal cues did you read to make you think this?	
What verbal cues did you read (think of the words they used and sounds made).	
Why may the person have felt this emotion?	
How did you respond verbally?	
How did you respond non-verbally?	
How might the individual have felt during and after your exchange?	
How might this exchange have been better – which aspects of inter and intra emotional intelligence can be improved?	

Self-efficacy

Self-efficacy is a belief that one can execute a given behaviour within a given setting (Knowles, Holton & Swanson, 1998).

> Self-efficacy is the belief in one's ability to perform a task and to have influence over events that affect one's life. Self-efficacy beliefs determine how people feel, think, motivate themselves and behave. The concept is much related to a person's sense of esteem and feelings about themselves.
> (Larkins, Westwood, Berry & Stone, 2014)

A self-efficacy questionnaire can identify those aspects of practice where the individual believes they are able to execute them confidently and also pinpoint those aspects requiring development (Parker, 2007). It is worth considering that individuals are not always the best judge of their own strengths and weaknesses because people are motivated to looking good and wishing to impress others with their abilities. It is, however, more likely that people underrepresent their abilities because they lack confidence, self-awareness or may not wish to boast. Therefore, an honest exchange with others can help to acknowledge areas of strength and the areas requiring development. Those supporting the learner or practitioner can assist in consolidating self-efficacy beliefs through providing skilled feedback and this is particularly important where one may have the skills but not the confidence in their ability.

Template 3.5 has been adapted from a tool devised by Jonathan Parker to identify perceptions of social work student competence during practice learning (Parker, 2006). The purpose of this template is to focus attention onto self-efficacy beliefs, to recognise strengths and identify areas for development. First, you need to make the template relevant to your own work practice and your manager or practice educator can help you to do this by writing pertinent statements. In Template 3.5 there are examples of statements to guide you. Edit, delete and add to the statements to ensure that the template is relevant to enable reflection upon confidence and abilities of emotional competence within the practitioner's own scope of practice. Therefore, the person writing the statements must word them in such a way as to show that the practitioner is focusing on their belief in their ability or competence to complete the behaviours or actions. The premise of this self-efficacy tool can of course be used to score other aspects of social work practice.

Template 3.5 Self-efficacy questionnaire

Provide a confidence score from 1 to 4 1 = very low confidence, 2 = low, 3 = confident, 4 = very confident	
How confident are you that you can work successfully with the following groups of people:	
Children with behavioural problems	
Parents of children with behavioural problems	
Children with medical illness	
Children who have been abused	
Parents of abused children	
Parents who have experienced domestic violence	
Perpetrators of domestic violence	
Children who have experienced parental separation	
Parents who have experienced separation	
Adolescents	
People with a mental illness	
Families of people with a mental illness	
People with a physical disability	
Families of people with a physical disability	
People with a life-threatening illness	
Families of people with a life-threatening illness	
Older people	
People from a different culture who speak English	
People from a different culture who do not speak English	
People who abuse alcohol	
People who abuse substances other than alcohol	
People who are loud, threatening, abusive or violent	
How confident are you that you can successfully:	
Establish contact with clients	
Form working relationships with clients	
Provide relevant information and advice	
Collect relevant information	
How confident are you that you can successfully:	
Write clear, explanatory and informative letters to clients	

(Continued)

Template 3.5 (*Continued*)

Write comprehensive, informative and relevant case notes	
Write comprehensive, informative and relevant assessment reports	
How confident are you that you can work successfully with:	
Other social work students	
Other social work staff	
Your supervisor/practice educator	
Administrative staff	
Other agency staff	
Teachers	
Health visitors	
Social workers external to the agency	
How confident are you that you can successfully:	
Apply theoretical models appropriately	
Identify learning needs	
Evaluate your practice	
Make plans to increase learning opportunities	
Recognise the ethical tensions inherent in the work	
How confident are you that you can successfully:	
Manage the stress that you will feel in a fast-paced working and learning environment	
Manage the frustration you will feel working within agency bureaucracy	
Manage the feelings that you will have working with clients experiencing emotional and psychological distress	
Manage the feelings you will have when clients or their families blame you for things going wrong	
Manage the feelings you will have when team members from other disciplines blame you for things going wrong	

Once the statements have been written, the practitioner scores their confidence against the statements and considers why they have scored it this way. Working with a peer or learning facilitator can stimulate dialogue to help unpack perceptions of confidence. Rather than leaving the exercise at that point the most important step is the action stage. Step three is to do something as a result of these insights. It is also advantageous to set a review date when the template can be completed again to see how perceptions of confidence may be different, remembering that sometimes when one becomes more proficient one tends to become harder on oneself and may score more harshly accordingly.

(I would like to extend a special thank you to Jonathan Parker for his permission to edit his template and for his contribution towards writing this guidance.)

Developing Emotional Intelligence in Supervision

Both formal and informal supervision are appropriate opportunities to work together to gain insight into and to work towards the development of emotional intelligence. However, learners with low levels of emotional intelligence may require more support to make the best use of supervision. Morrison (2005) suggests that 'supervisees with higher degrees of emotional competence will make more positive use of supervision' (Morrison, 2005:88). The implication here is that those in most need are less likely to maximise the benefits of supervision and therefore the skills of the supervisor are essential to create 'a secure and collaborative climate' (Morrison, 2005:57). The value of supervision for emotional support was highlighted by social workers themselves in research conducted by Hair (2013). The research data from the 636 social workers identified that 'the strongest reason for career-long supervision after graduation was for emotional support' (Hair, 2013:1577). Supervision is further explored in Chapter 7 and other reflective tools can be located throughout this book and in particular in Chapter 5.

Conclusion

Social workers need emotional intelligence to enable them to understand, manage and regulate their own emotions. They require emotional competence to act and respond appropriately in given situations. In addition to the intrapersonal aspect, practitioners also need emotional intelligence to manage the interpersonal dimension of working with and alongside others. Social workers need to be able to accurately read other peoples' emotions to competently interact with them and inform interventions. Those who are unable to read and respond appropriately to emotions will struggle to effectively communicate, engage and develop working relationships with service users, carers and other professionals.

As with all aspects of professional practice, social workers need to reflect upon emotional intelligence and work hard to develop insight and understanding about themselves and their ability to work alongside others. From initial training right through to those at the strategic level, all can reflect upon naturally arising experiences to fine-tune emotional intelligence. Reflecting upon, deepening insight into and developing emotional competence is required for all, regardless of their position within their social work career.

4
Developing Resilience for Effective and Safe Practice

Clare Stone

Introduction

Resilience is being able to adapt to internal and external stressors (Collins, 2007). It is also 'the ability to recover rapidly after experiencing some adverse experiences' (Saarni, 2000:81). Resilience is a term often used in social work practice as it is an 'emotionally and morally demanding' profession and practitioners need resilience and strategies to cope (Morrison, 2007:14).

Key Points

Resilience is being able to cope and deal with pressure and to not suffer longer-term consequences as a result. Social workers need resilience because:

- of the nature of the work they do,
- of the stresses caused by working in social work agencies, and
- they need to be able to do a professional job every day despite what is going on in their own private life.

Resilience is not a fixed attribute but can be developed by bolstering resources, and engaging in reflective practice and reflective supervision so as to develop coping strategies and self-efficacy.

Significance for Social Work Practice

Pressure at work can 'motivate us and enable us to perform at our best', however it is 'when we experience too much pressure without the opportunity to recover that we start to experience stress' (HSE, 2008:1). Stress is an adverse reaction that makes us unwell and ineffective in our role. Although some individuals appear to 'thrive' under a certain amount of pressure, by and large the stress of work can lead to burnout and impact upon the retention of social workers (Kinman & Grant, 2011:261).

The industries of 'human health and social work ... have statistically significantly higher estimated prevalence rates of work-related stress than across all industries averaged over 2010/11, 2011/12 and 2013/14' (HSE, 2014b:3). Research by McFadden (2015) found that 91 per cent of social workers have high levels of emotional exhaustion and 61 per cent depersonalisation (relating to compassion and responses to others) which puts them at high risk of burnout (McFadden, 2015). In social work we are exposed to daily pressures which can be summarised as arising from three main sources (Stone, 2014). First, the nature of social work can be challenging. Despite trying to work to promote a service user's well-being and safety, social workers are frequently met with hostility and aggression. Social work clients are often vulnerable, oppressed and face discrimination, and working to support such individuals can be stressful. The situations that workers face are often complex, traumatic and volatile.

> Social work involves working with people in distress and difficulties, people who have perhaps been traumatised by abuse or other life experience, people who have encountered major loss, suffering and pain. (Thompson, 2013:68)

The very nature of social work practice requires an individual to be resilient and this is sometimes referred to as emotional resilience. A second source of ongoing pressure comes from working within a social work agency where the pace of work can be relentless. The British Association of Social Work claims that almost one in ten social workers are considering leaving the profession because of high caseloads, excessive paperwork, lack of client contact time and budget cuts (BASW, 2014). Resilience is essential as social workers can 'struggle to cope with demands that are often unrelenting'

(Collins, 2007:256). There are demands and pressures because of the nature of doing social work tasks, but this is exacerbated by high levels of staff turnover, large caseloads, a lack of support and supervision, and ongoing resource constraints. Working within social work organisations is challenging.

The third aspect of resilience for social work practice relates to individuals being able to do this difficult job, despite what is going on in their own private lives. Regardless of external pressures the individual must turn up for work every day, on time and give it their full attention. Participants in research used examples from social work practice and student placements to construct the notion that without resilience an individual will not be able to cope and will therefore not be a safe or effective practitioner (Stone, 2014). In this research concern was expressed about an individual's capability for social work practice when issues from their private life (such as car trouble, childcare problems, ill health and relationship strains) impacted upon their practice.

Resilience to do the job of a social worker, in a social work agency and to manage both while balancing a private life requires resilience. As stated in the introduction to this book, the editors have a wealth of experience in supporting NQSWs and often hear them describe how they sometimes feel overwhelmed with the type and pace of work. One likened it to being on a treadmill and churning out assessments. Their reflections illustrate the resilience needed to be a social worker and operate within a social work agency. Many NQSWs express shock at the realities of front-line social work and others appear to thrive and enjoy the pressure. Carson, King & Papatraianou (2011) suggest that the theory of resilience can help us to understand why some social workers burnout from the stress of the work and then leave the profession (Carson et al., 2011).

Using in Practice

Resilience is not a fixed attribute; rather, it is an adaptive state that can be altered positively or negatively (Carson et al., 2011; Collins, 2007). Grant and Kinman (2013) argue that 'it is vital that social work students [and practitioners] learn that resilience is a quality that is not pre-determined, but one that can be developed through training and experience' (Grant & Kinman, 2013). Research suggests that those personality traits associated with resilience (such as positive emotionality, cultural and intellectual curiosity, friendliness, interpersonal confidence and organisation) are developed throughout initial training and while in practice (de las Olas Palma-García & Hombrados-Mendieta, 2014). The researchers go as far as to state:

> Based on this evidence, the development of activities and actions during university education and in the workplace that foster the development of these personality traits in social work students and social workers will contribute to making the individuals more resilient and will lead to improvements in their quality of life and ability to cope with adversity. (de las Olas Palma-García & Hombrados-Mendieta, 2014:11)

Their research, like that of Beddoe and colleagues (2014), adds weight to the idea that individuals ought to consider their own attributes to develop their resilient identities. In exploring practitioners' understanding of resilience, social workers 'identified the contribution of important practitioner attributes: openness and willingness to participate; reciprocal aid; courage to ask for assistance and the importance of self-reflection' (Beddoe, Davys & Adamson, 2014:123). They said it was important to utilise supervision and have collegial support but practitioners needed:

> to be open to learning, to listen, to ask for help, to accept and offer help, to acknowledge vulnerability, to be able to tolerate mistakes and to 'not know'. All these attributes enabled practitioners to access the resources and supports available. (Beddoe et al., 2014:124)

Researching resilience for social work Rajan-Rankin (2014) highlights internal and external changes in the development of self-identity and the 'acceptance of one's own emotions' as 'essential in order to develop a resilient and professional persona' (Rajan-Rankin, 2014:2438). Research is therefore indicating that resilience is developed via personality traits, attributes and where the individual is open to learning.

Although focusing on developing resilience in children, Lishman (2007) suggests that self-efficacy is an important dimension in the development of a resilient identity (Lishman, 2007). This is a useful concept because it is the recognition of one's strengths which develops the confidence to deal with future challenges (Wilks & Spivey,

2010). The individual who successfully copes with a difficult situation develops skills and internal confidence in their own abilities. The insight into one's ability to cope in pressured situations bolsters self-efficacy. Armed with new knowledge, skills and confidence, future situations are approached from a stronger position of internal resilience. Having the knowledge that you have resilience is a positive factor as it helps 'people to feel and to be more secure' (Payne, 2011:12). A self-efficacy exercise is included within Chapter 3.

It is suggested that greater resilience increases the ability to cope in adverse situations therefore developing 'resilience in social work students can ultimately impact their future success in the field' (Wilks & Spivey, 2010:286). Through auditing self-efficacy the student, the newly qualified and the more experienced social worker can recognise and develop resilience. A straightforward auditing process which Grotberg (1995) recommends for guiding the promotion of resilience, uses the following three headings of 'I have', 'I am' and 'I can' (Grotberg, 1995). Start by auditing those you have around you who offer you positive factors and then consider what you possess in terms of positive resilient attributes. Finally, identify the things you can do when support is provided (these may be internal attributes or external resources).

It is important to recognise that the key theme for the development of resilience is reflective practice. 'Reflective ability appears to be an important predictor of resilience and psychological well-being' (Kinman & Grant, 2011:261). Grant (2013) claims that those with high reflective abilities are able to avoid empathy distress, burnout and compassion fatigue (Grant & Rutsch, 2013). Kinman and Grant (2012) list ten factors to develop resilience which includes engaging in effective supervision (Kinman & Grant, 2012). Supervision must encourage the individual to explore critical reflection in a safe and supportive way as high quality supervision provides both support and a valuable context for learning (Carson et al., 2011). Social workers themselves agree that supervision contributes to well-being and resilience particularly when the relationship fosters safety and trust (Beddoe et al., 2014) (see Chapter 7 for further guidance on reflective supervision).

This process of developing a resilient self, requires a conducive and supportive environment where supervisors and educators also need to 'be in touch with their own emotionality and comfortable in addressing the emotional needs of' learners (Rajan-Rankin, 2014:2439). Those who support learners, whether in the university or in the workplace, need to consider how best to model resilience and create a safe and supportive environment in which the learner can develop their resilient identity. Employers have a responsibility here as individuals require regular nurturing and reflective supervision to develop emotions and optimism and to help 'establish and maintain resilience' (Collins, 2007:266). However, even when employers provide reflective opportunities the attributes of the social worker and their willingness to learn are required in order to maximise the learning potential within the supervisory relationship.

Although employers have a 'legal responsibility' for the wellbeing of staff this does not negate individual employee responsibility (Grant & Kinman, 2014:22). It is important for the individual to recognise when they are beginning to feel overwhelmed by pressure because failure to contain and manage pressure can lead to stress. Recognising what help is needed and what is the most appropriate form of support to draw upon helps to develop the resilient practitioner. Lishman (2007) also looks beyond the individual as she suggests that resilience can be encouraged 'by adding resources, bolstering and improving relationships and coaching people to develop skills that build self-efficacy' (Lishman, 2007:2005). Therefore, in addition to internal aspects, the social worker can also draw upon external sources as part of their 'resilience-building strategies' (Grant & Kinman, 2014:12). It is an individual's responsibility to ask for additional support and to work in collaboration with employers to avoid the development of stress and burnout.

Collins (2015) sums up the various elements to developing resilience for practice:

> Social work students and social workers cannot develop adequately without appropriate resources from agencies, support from colleagues, supervisors and professional development opportunities. Nevertheless, the ability to make challenge appraisals, to feel confident in their beliefs that they have valuable knowledge and skills and to feel they have some sense of control can help students and social workers become more self-directing, with a stronger commitment to their work and more likelihood of job satisfaction. Creative and intelligent use of the ideas surrounding appraisal, sense of coherence, self-efficacy and sense of control can offer hope and real possibilities for empowering social workers and social work students to become more confident and resilient practitioners, in both their current work and future careers. (Collins, 2015:81)

Case Study 4.1

Sylvia has specialised in working with older adults during her 15-year career. During this time she has developed extensive knowledge and skills in working with older adults, their families, carers and support services. She feels comfortable and confident in the work because she knows what resources there are in the geographical area and she has good working relationships with colleagues and values the support of managers. However, following a restructure Sylvia is now within an 'adult services' team where she works with all adults including those with a learning disability. Sylvia is feeling anxious and uncertain as she feels that she does not have the skills or knowledge required. She feels that the change to her work is unsettling, makes her feel less confident, reduces her satisfaction in work and ultimately impacts upon her resilience for practice.

Sylvia reflects alone, in supervision and with peers to explore her feelings and concerns. She uses the scaling exercise (see below) to identify how her resilience can be bolstered by drawing upon her existing skills and knowledge and considering the transferable nature of them. Sylvia recognises that she will need time and support to develop specific capabilities and awareness of resources so she therefore develops an action plan. The plan details training, includes supervision and arranging a mentor. Sylvia and her manager set a review schedule to monitor her increasing resilience and the effectiveness of the supporting strategies employed.

Case Study 4.2

Anselm is on his final social work placement, having excelled throughout the academic component and previous practice learning opportunity. He begins to feel that he is struggling to manage the competing demands on his time in terms of balancing the paperwork and being able to have meaningful contact time with the service user. As a result he feels under immense pressure and he questions his ability to maintain a high quality service and professionalism. Working long hours in order to complete work to a high standard is impacting on time with his family. Anselm begins to question his career choice as he feels unable to sustain his current level of work and balance the competing demands on his time from within and without the placement.

With his practice educator Anselm uses the bolstering confidence exercise (see next section) to identify a time when he previously coped well with pressure. Anselm reflects in depth and is able to recognise and celebrate a previous success and in doing so gains confidence in his abilities and reserves of resilience. He also identified what was particularly useful during that period which helped him to consider the resources and support required to help him complete his final placement.

Anselm began to prioritise by making decisions based upon the importance of the task and taking into account the time scales and standard of work required. He also reflected upon the scope of the social work role and how colleagues and other organisations can be drawn upon to support the service user; he learnt that he did not need to be all things to all people. To bolster his resilience for practice Anselm drew upon principles of time management, used task lists, spoke to his family about the demands he was facing and with them identified protected family time.

Bolstering Confidence

An important aspect of developing resilience is recognising a time when you coped well, as this can bolster your confidence for the future. Template 4.1 provides an activity that has been designed to encourage you to reflect in depth to celebrate a previous success with the intention of helping you have greater insight into your reserves and sources of support. Select a time in your life, moment or situation where you felt significantly under pressure or even stressed but you did manage to cope. This can be anything from your private or work life.

Template 4.1 Bolstering confidence

I faced a significant amount of pressure when:	
Emotionally I felt:	
How did my feelings impact on my behaviour, thought processes, health, professionalism, relationships?	
How might the other people have perceived/experienced me during this time?	
What was helpful during this period? Where did I draw strength from? (consider external and internal resources)	
What languages/words/phrases were particularly helpful?	

What behaviours/techniques/practices were particularly helpful?	
Looking back what have you learnt about yourself from this experience? (you may wish to consider emotions, behaviour, thoughts, practice)	
When faced with significant pressure I can/will…	

Building Resilience: Identifying and Managing Pressure to Avoid Stress

Social work is a high-pressured profession because of the nature of the work and the situations in which it is practised. However, all individuals cope with pressure in different ways and at different times. Rather than focus on the amount of pressures that we balance and manage, we need to attend to the impact that those pressures have on us as individuals. You need to be able to recognise when you are overwhelmed by the pressures.

This exercise will help you recognise when you are feeling unable to manage, unable to control and unable to respond appropriately. Most importantly it helps you identify the resources and support necessary to help bolster your resilience to cope with the pressure.

Step 1: Recognise the signs

There are early warning signs that we are becoming overwhelmed by pressure and at risk of stress. The Health and Safety Executive advise that 'if you are suffering from some of the following symptoms it may indicate that you are feeling the effects of stress' (HSE, 2014a):

Emotional symptoms

- Negative or depressive feeling
- Disappointment with yourself
- Increased emotional reactions – more tearful or sensitive or aggressive
- Loneliness, withdrawn

- Loss of motivation, commitment and confidence
- Mood swings (not behavioural)

Mental

- Confusion, indecision
- Unable to concentrate
- Poor memory

Changes from your normal behaviour

- Changes in eating habits
- Increased smoking, drinking or drug taking 'to cope'
- Mood swings affecting your behaviour
- Changes in sleep patterns
- Twitchy, nervous behaviour
- Changes in attendance such as arriving later or taking more time off (HSE, 2014a)

Make a note of emotional, mental and behavioural changes that occur when you feel like you are overloaded, unable to cope and overwhelmed. It may be useful to ask others to share their observations with you. 'Often, the people we are closest to can spot early warning signs of stress in us that we may not register ourselves' (Kinman, McMurray & Williams, 2014:160). Supervision is an appropriate environment in which to discuss your own personal early warning signs in order that your supervisor is alert to your support needs.

Step 2: Be specific about the cause of the stress

Make a note of the root cause(s). To help you identify the pressure(s) that is causing you to feel and become overwhelmed consider the prompts below:

- Work schedule: including hours of work, volume of work and targets. This can include lack of and slow pace of work.

- The type of work allocated. Confidence in your skills and abilities to do the work.
- Lack of recognition, reward and being valued for work.
- New practices, procedures or technology.
- Working relationships and conflict.
- Working environment and team culture.
- Expectations placed on you, job security, and uncertainties such as restructuring and workforce reorganisation.
- Management style and support from manager.
- Demands from outside the work setting (private life impacting on work).
- Health concerns.

Step 3: Existing support

Identify strategies, control measures and support that are already in place. Consider policies, procedures, training, supervision, Human Resources, induction, Occupational Health services, peers, buddy systems and other supportive networks. Make a note of how you can draw upon these existing resources and policies to help support you and reduce feeling overwhelmed by the pressures you identified in Step 2.

Step 4: Additional support

If you consider there is a gap in the existing support and control measures be very specific about what additional support you feel would be helpful. Now make a plan of how you are going to arrange for that support to be enacted. Set yourself clear aims and objectives.

Step 5: Monitor and review

It is essential that you review the support, resources and control measures that you have drawn upon and arranged. When will you review and how? Make a note of any third party who ought to be involved in reviewing the arrangements.

Part of the review may be to design an early warning plan. Consider what you will do when the signs of feeling overwhelmed (listed in Step 1) are next recognised. This is an important step in building your resilience for the profession.

You may find it helpful to use Template 4.2 to document your thoughts and outcomes from the five steps above.

Template 4.2 Building resilience

What are the signs of stress?	Be specific about the cause of stress	What is already in place to support me?	Additional support	Detail of the monitoring and review arrangements

Scaling Exercise

This exercise, at first glance, looks to be a simplified version of the exercise above, which helps you to identify how pressured you feel and so respond appropriately. However, you are not encouraged to engage in this activity in a superficial way. There is an opportunity to use this exercise to stimulate reflection and action for change using a solution-focused technique to bolster resilience. You may do this activity alone or use the prompts to engage in dialogue with another who can provide a confidential and supportive space for you to articulate your developing thoughts.

Begin by deciding how stressed you feel, with '0' representing no stress at all and '10' being the maximum pressure possible. Make a mark on the line below at the point that most closely represents how stressed and under pressure you feel. You need to explain why you have chosen that number.

0 ——————————— 5 ——————————— 10

The next step is to conceptualise and articulate reducing that 'stress' score by one or two points. Imagine that you scored your present stress level at 6, now ask yourself what would it look like to be at 4? What would it feel like to be at 4? What would other people notice about you if you were at 4? What strengths do you already have and can draw upon to reach this position? What strategies and resources do you have to make that change a reality?

These questions encourage you to focus on the strengths and solutions at your disposal and to move in a more positive direction. Although the causes of the pressures may be complex, your solutions do not necessarily have to be so.

This line exercise combines a number of techniques and theories for change. You need to engage in honest reflection (alone or with another), focus on the solution and use a strengths perspective through recognising and enacting your situated power. An important aspect of being resilient is self-awareness and identifying your own strengths. The strengths approach is a practice methodology which 'imbues a sense of possibility' (Oko, 2011:110). Identifying strengths rather than deficiencies and recognising you have the ability to bolster resilience is empowering.

Using the Principles of Cognitive Behavioural Theory

The principle of cognitive behavioural theory is helpful in the development of resilience because it pays attention to the relationship between thinking and behaviour. 'Cognitive behavioural therapy explores how systematic thinking styles, particularly thinking errors, have a significant impact on how experiences and events are perceived' (Grant & Kinman, 2014:96). Therefore, in times of pressure, if negative and unhelpful perspectives are holding us back we may limit our ability to cope and perform to our maximum potential. As perceptions and responses are connected, the aim is to break the negative cycle of counterproductive thinking and behaviour to a more positive modified thinking-response relationship. This exercise and Template 4.3 have been designed to encourage you to recognise negative thoughts, to employ reframing techniques and to consider practical approaches to advance your mindset. The exercise is based upon the principle that, within cognitive behavioural therapy, there are five areas to address:

- situations
- thoughts
- emotions
- physical feelings
- actions (NHS, 2014)

Like the majority of activities in this book you can do the exercise alone or with a trusted 'other'.

Begin by thinking about the situation in which you feel overwhelmed. What negative thoughts do you have and how do they impact on your emotional state, your physical feelings and your actions? You may be able to recognise a counterproductive negative relationship between thinking and behaviour that is difficult to break. 'Rather than accept this way of thinking you could accept ... learn ... and move on, and feel optimistic about the future' (NHS, 2014:1). By honestly acknowledging feelings and breaking the problem down the aim is to begin to address the issues and to reconstruct alternatives.

The next step is to determine what is particularly unhelpful about your thinking, in order to begin the journey to a more helpful and productive conceptualisation. Challenging unhelpful thoughts and behaviours is not easy and may take time and motivation. Use those around you to help identify the links and work out alternatives. Reframing thoughts is not instantaneous and you will need to work at this; you will need to practise. However, by recognising the link between counterproductive thinking and behaviour at this point in time may be a helpful way to develop your resilient identity to avoid the negative downward spiral when you are next beginning to recognise the signs of becoming overwhelmed and under pressure. Next time you may be better positioned to identify and acknowledge counterproductive negative cognitions which limit the way you think and lead to the identification of strengths and thereby the development and adoption of alternative positive productive thoughts and behaviours.

You may find the chapters on critical reflection through narrative constructions and coaching particularly useful to assist you to work through the stages in this exercise. Template 4.3 provides the main questions from the exercise above, which uses the principles of cognitive behavioural theory to develop resilience. You can use Template 4.3 to record your developing thinking or alternatively the questions may be drawn upon and used as prompts during reflective discussion.

Template 4.3 Developing resilience through cognitive change

What negative thoughts do you have and how do they impact on your emotional state, physical feelings and your actions?	
What is particularly unhelpful about your thinking?	
What is a more helpful way of thinking/ how can you reframe negative thoughts?	
What learning do you take forward for the future?	

Conclusion

Social work can be a very rewarding profession and practitioners have the privilege of engaging with individuals who are inspiring, interesting and motivating. However, social workers also work alongside individuals who are disadvantaged, angry and in crisis. Practitioners have to attempt to engage people who do not welcome their interventions and others who may be in dire need of support and want social work help yet find that access to appropriate resources to support them can prove challenging. To do the difficult job of social work, resilience is required. A social worker needs to be resilient to work with those who use social work services. They need resilience to work in social work services where there are limited resources to help service users and the social workers themselves may receive less than adequate support to do the role effectively. To work within these two levels of pressure and balance a home life also requires resilience.

In social work there are a range of pressures from a range of sources and some individuals cope well with these. However, when the pressure begins to impact on the ability to perform, practitioners begin to experience stress which can lead to ill health and burnout, and result in some individuals leaving the profession. As practitioners we have little, if any, influence in eradicating inequality at the societal level; impacting on the availability of resources; or protecting services users from the effects of the ageing process or from contracting illness. However, at an individual level social workers can identify their internal strengths and draw upon resources and support to bolster their resilience to do the best social work practice they can.

5
Engaging in Reflective Practice

Clare Stone

Introduction

In social work we frequently use the term 'reflection' as shorthand for acknowledging the need to stop and think about something or to suggest that we have indeed thought a bit more deeply about a particular issue. The terms self-reflection, reflexivity and critical reflection are often used interchangeably and the following basic definitions may help in seeing the similarities and differences between these terms.

Self-reflection can also be called 'reflexivity' and it means to focus on the self. Illeris (2002) suggests that 'no clear boundary can be drawn between personal development and reflexivity, but one could perhaps say that personal development increasingly takes place through reflexivity' (Illeris, 2002:95). This is because reflexivity is self-reflection and akin to looking into a mirror with the purpose of self-analysis. The aim of this self-analysis is to assist in understanding oneself and to generate new insights for learning and self-development. This is essential for social workers, as they need to make links between what they do and why they do it, and maintain a continuous focus on their professional self. For example, social workers can ask themselves why they felt particularly anxious in a given situation, why do they find it easier to establish professional relationships with mothers rather than fathers, or the social worker may reflect on how they structured the questions that resulted in the service user asking them to leave their property. The purpose here is to understand the use of self, understand how one's history and experiences shape current practice, or as Gilbert and Sliep (2009) suggest, this type of self-reflexivity is 'a critical appraisal of self-in-action' (Gilbert & Sliep, 2009:468). In summary, it is asking: 'What do I do, why do I do it that way and what is the impact?' The purpose is to inform change to develop the professional self and practice.

Self-reflection and reflexivity look at our own being whereas critical reflection encourages the practitioner to look more widely at how other things influence and impact practice:

> Critical reflection calls into question the power relationships that allow, or promote, one set of practices considered to be technically effective. It assumes that the minutiae of practice have embedded within them the struggles between unequal interests and groups that exist in the wider world. For reflection to be considered critical it must have as its explicit focus uncovering, and challenging, the power dynamics that frame practice and uncovering and challenging hegemonic assumptions (those assumptions we embrace as being in our best interests when in fact they are working against us). (Brookfield, 2009:293)

To be critically reflective one needs to consider the power relations at play, the cultural influences, political ideologies, and the influence of community, family and environment. Rather than just make a referral to a food bank, a critically reflective practitioner may question why in the twenty-first century there is a need for food banks in Britain. The critically reflective social worker will question the ramifications and impact of their statutory duties and legislative frameworks on those they work with, families and communities. There is further discussion about critical reflection in Chapter 6 which is entitled 'Advanced critical reflection through narrative (re)construction'.

Self-reflection and critical reflection are often compressed and we talk in social work about critically reflective practice that focuses on the self within the wider contexts for practice. For this chapter the simple term 'reflection' is adopted to represent the social worker thinking about the use of self while taking into consideration the wider critical aspects which may also have a bearing on practice. Reflection is an appropriate term because the social worker is encouraged to consider all elements that impact upon their own development and the service that they deliver.

Key Points

Reflecting on practice is important for self-development and to ensure the quality of the service provided. Having an experience alone does not mean that learning has taken place. Analysing components of the experience to consider the what, how and why of social work practice can provide insight into how good practice can be replicated, and where and how improvements can be made. Reflection, therefore, is looking at one's own knowledge, skills and values alongside analysis of wider aspects which impact on practice, such as discrimination, legislation and society.

Reflective practice:

- requires the practitioner to focus on what they are doing and why they are doing it, and to be consciously attentive to the impact.
- focuses attention onto our practice to celebrate strengths and highlights areas for development;
- can be done alone or with the support of others such as peers, an educator or supervisor;
- requires time, motivation and commitment; and
- is essential during initial training and throughout one's career as it draws attention to safe and effective social work practice.

Significance for Social Work Practice

Social workers need to engage in reflective practice as social work is a profession that requires lifelong learning. As a student graduates from initial training they will not have all the knowledge and skill requirements to see them safely through their entire career. Learning from initial training needs to be consolidated and the individual needs to continue to learn and develop. They need to enhance and improve within the three pillars of social work practice: knowledge, skills and values. Social work is ever changing and, therefore, practitioners need to update their abilities. One way to do this is through formal training, and another is through reflecting on experiences. 'Practice wisdom' is a term often used in social work which means to apply knowledge through an appropriate use of the self (Thompson & West, 2013). Practice wisdom is having the formal knowledge but intuitively drawing upon it and applying it appropriately in unique practice situations. The knowledge part of practice wisdom can be taught but what to do with it 'can only be learned through real life experiences' (Thompson & West, 2013:119). To have practice wisdom and therefore be wise in practice requires one to have these life experiences, to reflect on them and to learn from them. Wise practitioners will then aim to replicate the things that went well, improve those aspects that need developing and identify ongoing learning needs. It is helpful to think of reflection as a cyclical process where one considers what is already known, then have the experience from which they learn with the aim of improving practice (Kolb, 1984; Schön, 1991). Imagine the electrical technician who comes to mend an appliance in your home and on blowing it up remarks 'oh! The last one like this I tried to mend also blew up.' One expects a professional to learn and advance their practice rather than repeating mistakes, failing to improve and failing to advance their abilities. Like the technician, social workers also need to approach practice from an informed situation and continually develop their knowledge, skills and values. In the cyclical learning process similar to Kolb's experiential learning and the reflective circle of Schön, the learner prepares for an activity and the next step is for them to engage in an experience (Kolb, 1984; Schön, 1991). The reflective cycle concludes with the learner reflecting on experience and considers how practice can be improved by drawing upon wider theory and feedback. The aim of the cycle is to learn from experience and improve by amending practice. It is important for social workers to reflect to ensure that they are aware of their strengths and areas for development. In addition to professional development, reflecting on the service delivered is also important to ensure that service users obtain the best service possible.

Using in Practice

Any experience has the potential to be a learning opportunity but it is important for the practitioner to be honest, open to learning and motivated. Honest self-analysis of strengths and those areas that require development is not always easy to achieve. Practitioners can request feedback from others such as peers, supervisors and, of course, service users to validate perspectives and add alternative insights into one's abilities. However, this requires being open to learning as reflective practice can expose aspects of vulnerability. Therefore, to actively seek feedback, to analyse self and then to make changes as a result of new insights requires strong motivation. Reflective practice is not a passive indulgent activity but ought to be dynamic and responsive. Developing an action plan can be a useful framework for identifying what needs to be changed, how you are going to address this, the timescale, and also for the recording of the support and resources you require (see Template 5.4).

Often we think back to situations and replay events over and over in our head and take the time to consider how some aspects could have been done differently. This is reflecting, but in an informal unstructured way, and there is less chance that transformative practice will result. Therefore, this chapter offers a range of templates to prompt more structured reflection. The templates have a great deal of similarity but are all slightly different and therefore individuals may select as they see appropriate. Feel free to use the templates as they are presented here or take bits from a number of templates, mix them up and even add in additional sections and questions. The most important thing is to reflect in depth upon an aspect of practice to help develop insight and understanding into current skills, knowledge and values with the purpose of identifying further learning needs. The aim of active dynamic and responsive reflection is to work towards becoming a more insightful and capable practitioner.

Reflection can be an activity undertaken alone or with others. The templates included in this chapter can be used in a number of ways; for example, they can be used by an individual as a solitary activity and kept private, or insights can be shared with a trusted other (for example, in supervision). The prompts on the templates can be used to structure questions to begin a reflective dialogue. In this latter application it is important to remain focused on the practitioner's reflection rather than spending too long describing the practice scenario. Practitioners can easily become distracted as they discuss an interesting complex practice situation and can find their time is used up through concentrating on the detail of the case rather than reflecting on themselves as developing practitioners. The same distractions can occur in group reflection and therefore it is important to provide clear instruction and establish parameters for the participants.

Reflective writing and keeping a reflective diary is common practice for social workers and students but often many will fail to go beyond providing an overly descriptive account. It is important for those doing reflective writing to engage in the analytical components of reflection. Whether people are writing individual reflective accounts or keeping a reflective diary it is essential to briefly consider what has happened but then they must move on to elaborate on what has been learnt from that experience and identify how practice can be developed. Any of the templates below can be used as a framework for reflective writing and diary-keeping.

The main purpose of all of these templates is to encourage reflection and as outlined above select the parts that are meaningful to the individual or to the situation and amend the format as needed. However, when using reflective templates remember to follow the complete reflective cycle and attempt to work towards replicating the good aspects of practice and also to make changes as a result of new insights. Thinking is not enough; reflection is not just replaying an incident in your head or chatting about it. Reflection is concerned with analysis to inform learning and development.

> Case Study 5.1
>
> Sharon Scott was a social work student at the time of writing but her level of reflection and analysis can inspire students, early career social workers and those who are more experienced. Through honest and insightful reflection, Sharon considers how her own views and understandings may relate to the public construction of asylum seekers and those with disabilities.
>
>> During initial engagement with Mrs W, I experienced a great deal of empathy with her both in respect of the frustration she expressed in relation to having been denied extra financial support to care for her disabled son, and also more broadly in respect of her experience of poverty and oppression. As the intervention has developed however, I have begun to question the validity and reliability of some of what Mrs W has shared with me in respect of her son's disability, and more generally with regards to her various claims for welfare benefits both on the basis of 'gut feelings' and in response to information from other sources.
>>
>> Mrs W's potential dishonesty presents some dissonance with regards to my own personal values in relation to the importance of honesty and integrity, and also presents some issues for me as to what would motivate someone to knowingly seek to have their child 'labelled' as being disabled.
>>
>> In reflecting upon my feelings with regards to Mrs W's level of honesty I acknowledge that, as a result of having worked for a protracted period of time within a largely risk led environment with a focus on the application of critical analysis to information shared by service users, I have developed some propensity for scepticism in this regard.
>>
>> Furthermore, I am aware that in assessing the reliability of the information presented by Mrs W in respect of her circumstances, I have drawn upon my knowledge in relation to non-verbal cues - for example, her capacity to maintain eye contact - and there is some evidence within this that would generally

be suggestive of dishonesty. I acknowledge however that my understanding of non-verbal cues is framed within the context of my own cultural experience and that such cues may have different meaning within other cultures.

I have also considered how far the current political debate in respect of immigration and the recent media representations of people arriving in the UK from Eastern Europe may have influenced my perceptions of Mrs W. Whilst I choose to engage with media that I believe to present balanced and evidenced views and would never knowingly engage in stereotyping individuals or groups of people, I would contend that the constant bombardment of negative portrayals of particular societal groups across the media has the potential to permeate the subconscious. In recognising this, it would seem critical as I continue to work with Mrs W that I practise with a conscious awareness of 'self' in identifying any external forces that may potentially influence my perceptions of others.

In reflecting upon my concerns in respect of Mrs W knowingly seeking to have one of her children labelled as being disabled, I am aware that these are underpinned by my own cultural understanding of disability and my own personal experience of how oppressive and disempowering such a label can be, even within a society that purports to value disabled individuals and treat them equally. Whilst I have some understanding of Mrs W's motivations in making the claim for DLA for her child, it would seem to me that her son is already socially and materially disadvantaged within society as a result of his minority ethnic status and that labelling him as being disabled could potentially exclude him further, a concept with which I struggle.

In the edited passage Sharon is self-reflecting on her developing professional self and also reflecting upon the personal/psychological, cultural and social/structural layers of discrimination (Thompson, 1993). As an academic I have read many bland reflective statements such as 'I worked in a person-centred way to empower him' and the more concerning one 'I used the task-centred model on him to share power' without being able to decipher what informed that practitioner's practice nor whether they had adequate insight into the complex compositions of practice. The templates in this chapter aim to help you go deeper, be clearer about the 'what', the 'why' and the 'how' of social work and also to explore an individual's positionality as a practitioner.

Reflection on Practice

The aim of Template 5.1 is for practitioners to engage in reflective thinking about social work practice, social work process, knowledge, values, skills and professional development. The template requires the social worker to reflect on what they are doing and why. It is the analysis that requires critical thinking but the event itself does not need to be critical: it does not need to be dramatic, extraordinary or a crisis. The event upon which you reflect and analyse can be any element of your social work practice and its influences, and examples include an agency procedure, a way of working, a case, a meeting, a social issue or legislation. Therefore, the analysis can consider the routine and the typical, rather than the extraordinary and the challenging. Although depth of thinking is essential, lengthy description is not required; the emphasis is on depth of reflective analysis and the quality of the inclusions rather than the amount of writing. In collaboration with a group of practitioners and drawing upon the work of Harry Douglas, I devised a similar template for use with initial training students within the Greater Lancashire Social Work Education and Training Network (Douglas, 2008). The template was further developed by the two editors of this book to encourage deeper reflection with early career social workers. I have included here, as Template 5.1, a simplified version which has guidance and prompts within it to aid the learning process.

Template 5.1 Reflection on practice

Pseudonym(s) of service user(s)/carer(s) used
A brief outline of the presenting scenario at the point at which you were asked to undertake the intervention
Try to minimise description but highlight <u>the main issue</u> that you are going to focus on. Examples to illustrate this: ➢ B has learning disabilities and his mother expressed concern about him going out in the evenings and therefore I undertook a risk assessment (the focus of the analysis will be about balancing risk and independence). ➢ The application for continuing care for Mrs Jones was rejected and I had to discuss alternative care arrangements with her family (the focus of the analysis is on policy, legislation and the principles of integrated care). ➢ I was allocated a child protection referral and was very anxious as this was my first one (the analysis considers developing confidence and use of professional authority). ➢ The agency has introduced a new IT system which is delaying the authorisation of support for service users (the focus of the analysis is the impact of practice on the users of the service). **You may therefore focus on a case or alternatively focus on a practice issue and use case(s) to illustrate the points you make**

What were the objectives of the intervention? (bullet points are acceptable)
You can be really specific here about what it is you are trying to achieve, examples may be: To advocate for Mr Z in a multi-professional meeting. To ensure that I work within the Community Care (Delayed Discharge) Act 2003. To support R during the foster placement move. **Numbering the objectives (if you list more than one) will help you refer back to them later in the document.**
What was the mandate for your practice? Please consider your responsibilities with reference to legislation, national and local policies and procedures.
It is expected that relevant legislation or guidance will be listed and that you will detail the social worker role and responsibilities. Therefore don't just name the act but state how this informs what you need to do/legal responsibilities.
Theories to inform. What theories do you draw upon to help you understand the service user and their situation?
Think about how theory (knowledge and research) helps you to make sense of the family or the individual's situation (theory to inform). Don't just list theories but explain their relevance.
Strategies for intervention. What social work methods and theory inform your interventions and help you work towards achieving the aims & objectives as detailed above?
Think about what theories, knowledge areas, research, models of practice inform your interventions. Don't just make a list because you need to explain their relevance.
Self-awareness: What were your own feelings about this situation?
You may include in this self-reflection section anything that you wish in relation to your professional development or professional identity. For example you may consider knowledge, skills, values, biases, resilience for practice, emotional competence or feelings. *Take care not to drift into thoughts about the situation as this self-awareness is about you as the practitioner.*
Tuning in: What might the service user's possible feelings be about:
The agency, you, and the situation? Please consider the impact of the intervention on the service user.
How does it feel to be a service user of this service? What is your understanding of their experience within this situation/service/arrangement? Draw upon verbal and non-verbal cues to evidence and support your opinion.
What ethical considerations did you encounter?
Consider the balance of professional rights and responsibilities and how this links to legislative considerations, sector standards and professional codes where relevant. It may be appropriate to consider the service user group and their potential vulnerabilities, discrimination through policy or different professionals' perspectives.

(Continued)

Template 5.1 (*Continued*)

Critically appraise your intervention with reference to legislation, policy, theory, knowledge, research and social work methods.
This requires you to go beyond stating whether you achieved your aims and making bland statements such as 'I followed guidance and worked in a person-centred way.' Consider the strengths and limitations of the intervention, drawing upon policy or knowledge/research, concluding whether the theory behind the practice matched the reality of the intervention.
Reflecting on your experience, identify three things you did well. (bullet points are acceptable)
Reflecting on your experience, identify areas for development in terms of your professional practice. (bullet points are acceptable)
How do you plan to address these developmental areas? (bullet points are acceptable)

Reflective Questions

Template 5.2 illustrates the five simple questions form the basis of reflecting upon practice. They can be used as a template to structure reflective writing (such as a reflective diary) or as verbal prompts to guide reflective discussions.

Template 5.2 Reflective questions

What?	
Who?	
Why?	
How?	
Where?	

Here are examples of how these five questions can be further broken down. It is important to keep the description very brief but elaborate on the analysis.

What?

What did you want/aim to achieve?

What did happen?

What helped?

What hindered/did not help?

Who?

Who does this impact on?

Who else may have been influenced?

Who else may have assisted?

Why?

Why did you want/aim to achieve that?

Why did X happen?

Why did that help?

Why did that hinder/make things worse?

How?

How do you know that? (draw upon verbal and non-verbal feedback to check out your analysis)

How do you feel about X?

How can you make X happen again?

How can you avoid X happening again?

Where?

Where do you go from here?

This is the stage where you draw up an action plan and you may want to use the same prompts:

What is it you wish to achieve as a result of this reflective insight?

Why is this important (for you, your service/employer and for service users)?

How are you going to work on this?

Who can support you?

The Reflective Cycle

Figure 5.1 incorporates the principle of a reflective cycle as discussed earlier in the chapter. Begin the cycle for the first time at the experience stage and use the prompts to focus upon the 'what', 'why' and then 'what next'. You can use the prompts in Figure 5.1 during dialogue or remove the additional text and use the cyclical illustration as a reflective template to write on.

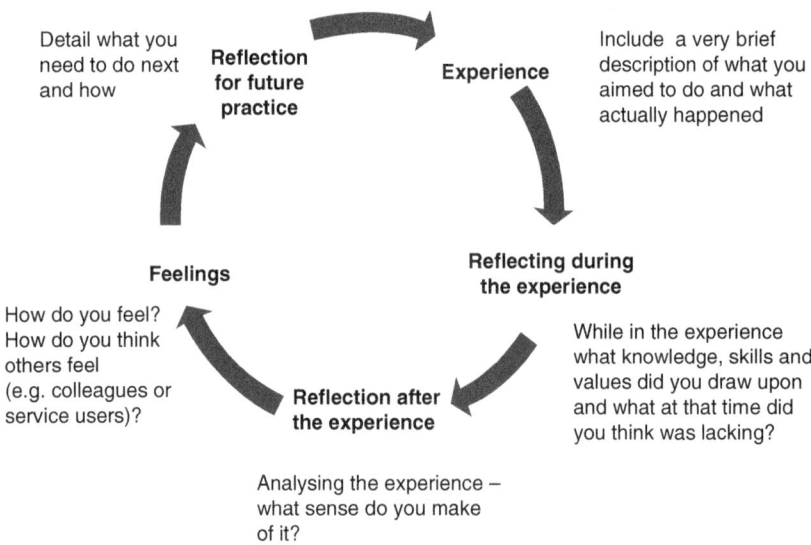

Figure 5.1 Reflective cycle

Reflecting on a Learning Activity

When you have undertaken an activity it is important to reflect upon the value of that experience in terms of ongoing learning. The learning activity can be any experience that you have and may include, for example, watching a video, reading a book, shadowing a colleague or attending formal training. Template 5.3 provides structure for reflecting on a learning activity with the aim of developing practice and shaping future learning.

Template 5.3 Reflecting on a learning activity

Identify three things that resonated with you (rang a bell, made you think) during this learning activity 1) 2) 3)
What have you learnt from this activity?
What is the significance of these points to your role?
How will you incorporate this learning into your work/practice? (amend your practice, implement new learning or develop knowledge)
What further learning do I need?
Where will I find the information?
Other notes

Using Art to Reflect

Art can be a useful medium to encourage reflection on positive and negative emotions, experiences and thoughts. Learners can use pictures from the internet or magazines, draw or paint, or even take photographs to capture images that reflect their internalised feelings. In a safe and supportive environment they then describe what the art form represents and the aim of this is to encourage deeper insight and reflection. Mulder and Aubrey (2014) used photographs and narrative during initial training to 'focus inward to ask students to explore their own thoughts and values about social work' (Mulder & Aubrey, 2014:1018). Lectures invited those training to be teachers to create collages and write a reflective piece to encourage them to explore both the experience 'and those factors that played a significant role in shaping …[the] students' perceptions of experience' (MacKenzie & Wolf, 2012:6). Trainee doctors have been 'encouraged to seek out exhibits which resonated with a clinical encounter or experience' and then write a reflective piece (Thresher et al., 2013:212). Art can be a useful medium to stimulate reflection in students but it can also be used with all social work learners and can be used with groups, pairs or as a sole activity.

There are different ways to use art to aid reflection. For example the learner may have questions to answer using a visual medium:

- Which values do you consider most important for social workers?
- What experiences from your past do you consider define who you are today?

The learner may also be given a title to focus and structure their artistic reflection such as:

- The rewards of being a social worker.
- The balance of care and control within social work practice.

Giving parameters in advance of the art activity enables the practitioner learner to think about the images they wish to capture and this in itself is a reflective and analytical process because it focuses the thoughts inwards, or on practice and can develop self-awareness.

Developing a Reflective Learning Action Plan

As discussed throughout this chapter reflection does not stop at the point of analysing what happened. It is essential that the consideration of what happened and why is used as a spur for learning, development and for the improvement of practice. Template 2.1 introduced in Chapter 2 provides a useful structure to help focus upon what needs to be learnt, how it will be learnt, assessment, support and review. That template can be used to ensure that attention is given to learning and development within reflective practice. However, you may wish to devise a learning plan to ensure that you give thought to how you can make time to reflect. The first thing to decide is how often you will do structured reflection but remember this timed reflective exercise is in addition to the more spontaneous and ongoing reflection. Template 5.4 has text included to stimulate your thinking and this example here prompts the practitioner learner to undertake at least one formal reflective activity per month. Use Template 5.4 to plan for and commit to reflection.

Template 5.4 Reflective learning action plan

When will I reflect?	How will I reflect?	What support/ resources do I need?	Additional notes
January	I will take time to reflect on one recent practice experience using Template 5.1: 'Reflection on practice'	Template 5.1	This can be used within my evidence of engaging in ongoing learning/CPD activities for professional re-registration
February	I will engage in a reflective discussion	I will invite X (a colleague) to have coffee and to engage in a reflective dialogue	We both need to agree parameters and purpose

Conclusion

Although we have theories to draw upon, research to inform practice, laws outlining responsibilities and rights, and practice guidance, social work is complex and the use of self is a powerful tool which shapes our interventions. It is essential for social workers to be aware of what they are doing and why they are doing it, and be consciously attentive to the impact of their practice on others. Therefore, reflective practice is key to safe and effective social work practice. Reflective practice focuses attention onto our practice and highlights areas for development. It is essential that reflection is an ongoing and career-long aspect of practice. The tools in this chapter are offered to trigger reflective thinking but it is for the individual to find what works best for them. This includes carving out protected time to reflect, either alone or with the support of another.

6
Advanced Critical Reflection Through Narrative (Re)Construction

Clare Stone

Introduction

This learning methodology involves constructing, deconstructing and reconstructing a narrative to explore dominant ways of thinking with the aim of bringing about change. Put simply, this involves speaking about something from practice with the aim of better understanding those aspects that hinder progress, and these insights are used to consider a more advantageous way of re-approaching one's practice. The narrative approach can identify positive aspects of practice but the main purpose is to expose the discourses that have a negative influence. In social work we may find that previous training and experiences do not adequately equip us to 'manage the uncertainty and complexity' of a practice situation (Fook & Gardner, 2007:9). We therefore need to critically reflect in order to expose the challenges and dominant ways of thinking so as to provide the opportunity to reconstruct more advantageous language, approaches and strategies for social work intervention. This type of reflection is best described as critical reflection as it 'calls into question the power relationships that allow, or promote, one particular set of practices over others' (Brookfield, 2009:294). Brookfield (2009) draws attention to 'power dynamics and relationships' within critical reflection:

> Becoming aware of how the dynamics of power permeates all professional practice helps us realise that forces present in the wider society always intrude into our work with clients and colleagues. Critical reflection regards social work practices, professional and ethical codes, and accepted modes of decision-making as contested. (Brookfield, 2009:300)

This critically reflective approach aims to expose dominant assumptions and the power within relationships with a view to challenging and changing them (White, Fook & Gardner, 2006). However, like all transformative learning this approach requires one to engage in deep reflection, to be honest, to have a commitment to learn and then change practice as a result of that learning. Authoring and re-authoring narratives can be emotionally taxing and can expose fears and uncertainties, therefore to do this safely it requires time, a conducive environment and the support of a supervisor, educator or trusted critical friend.

Key Points

Whereas self-reflection considers the individual's direct practice and own being, critical reflection encourages the practitioner to look beyond self to such things as power relations, culture, politics, and other aspects such as community, family and environment which may impact practice. By examining speech one can begin to have some insight into how our perspectives of these domains limit our practice and the intention is to reconstruct an alternative approach. Advanced critical reflection through narrative (re)construction requires:

- Engagement in both critical reflect and self-reflection.
- The support of a facilitator to help deconstruct and reconstruct the narrative.
- Commitment to challenge dominant ways of thinking.
- Motivation to begin to consider alternative practices.

Significance for Social Work Practice

The depth of critical reflection in narrative methodology may enable social workers to 'respond to the many social problems requiring active, creative and critical responses, by helping them to transform their thinking about change and how it can be achieved' (Morley, 2013:14). The practitioner is afforded a safe space to unpick how they approach a situation with a view to re-approaching it from a more informed and powerful stance. The situation upon which we critically reflect can be anything and examples may include working with an individual service user, a family, a community, working within a policy framework or collaborating with other professionals.

Critical reflection through narrative construction can also be a useful learning tool for students to begin to understand themselves, to develop self-efficacy and become a more competent practitioner (Gibson, 2012). Gibson's approach requires the student to focus on self in order to reconstruct a less negative narrative which builds upon their strengths rather than them becoming stifled by focusing on weaknesses and limitations. A student can utilise feedback from service users and colleagues to assist and encourage them to celebrate their strengths and achievements while they undertake practice-learning placements. The 'narrative approach can be an empowering method as it allows students to take control over the direction of their practice as they can start to re-author their own stories' (Gibson, 2012:62). This is echoed by Kearns and McArdle (2012) who advocate the use of narrative learning as it centres power with the learner (Kearns & McArdle, 2012). The centring of power with the narrator is therefore a useful methodology to aid critical reflection within initial social work education but can also be used as a strategy to inform interventions with the users of social work services. The social worker can use this as an empowering strategy with services users to construct, deconstruct and reconstruct their own narratives. Advanced critical reflection through narrative (re)construction is a person-centred technique designed to bolster self-awareness with the ultimate aim of making changes and therefore has relevance with many aspects of social work practice. Although this learning methodology can be employed with service users and students the remainder of this chapter explores the use of the narrative approach to 'enable practitioners to envision possibilities for change' within their own practice (Morley, 2013:2).

Using in Practice

To begin with, the individual (referred to in this chapter as the social worker) tells their trusted critical friend (the facilitator) about a situation from practice. This can be any practice experience and examples may include where one felt challenged, deskilled, blocked or unable to see a way forward. The social worker 'presents a "story", or *their version* of what happened' in relation to the crucial incident (Fook &

Gardner, 2007:82 italics in original). The facilitator may prompt and ask questions to tease out the tensions, the challenges and the social worker's perspectives to aid deeper understanding. 'Storytelling is a relational activity' as the facilitator encourages the narrator to tell their story and the duo must feel comfortable working together (Riessman, 2001:697). Consideration also ought to be given to the environment as the social worker must consider it to be a safe and supportive space in which they feel empowered to speak freely.

The social worker telling their story about something from practice is the narrative construction stage (the first stage) and the dialogue between the social worker and facilitator may be audio recorded.

The second stage is to deconstruct the narrative and this is where listening back to an audio recording may be useful. The deconstruction process is the interpreting and analysing of the narrative and this may take place immediately or at a later point in time. As one becomes more familiar with the methodology, the deconstruction of narrative may occur while the narrative is being spoken. This is because social workers are skilled interviewers who deconstruct, assess, interpret and analyse during conversation and these skills will be spontaneously deployed. The social worker and facilitator may use a template (see template 6.1) to help deconstruct and make a record of their developing thoughts.

The aim of the deconstruction process is to identify the discourses of 'everyday activities and interactions' as experienced and constructed by the social worker (Miller & Fox, 2004:36). This brings to one's attention the dominant ways of thinking which have exacerbated the challenges in relation to the activity being reflected upon. It may help to think of the deconstruction stage like the process we undertake when we try to understand a play or some other performance (Riessman, 2001). To understand what is going on in the play we need to know about the relationships between the characters, the power struggles, the history and the plots that shape the story. So to translate this to narrative deconstruction we ask where the social worker positions themselves in relation to other characters and plots in the story. Are they 'victims of one circumstance or another in their stories, giving over to other characters rather than themselves the power' or do they 'assume control over events and actions' and we may ask whether they give 'themselves active roles in certain scenes and passive roles in others' (Riessman, 2001:702). To identify and begin to unpack the discourses at play, it is important to pay particular attention to the language structures the narrator has drawn upon and consider:

- What words are used in their narrative to describe the people and practices?
- Where does the social worker situate power: what are the power relationships that are experienced?
- What are the factors that limit progress?
- Do they speak of rules and practices that constrain/prohibit?

By critically analysing the narrative in this way we are attending to the structures that comprise our practice. This depth of deconstructing the narrative facilitates consideration of the discourses both within practice and that surround one's practice. 'Discursive formation' is structured by 'beliefs and practices, words and things' (McNay, 1994:69). Critical analysis begins with the awareness of discursive constructions, which stimulates the process of thought for finding alternative approaches to practice. The elements that comprise a discourse are not fixed for all time and can therefore be modified and changed. Put simply, by recognising the way the story has been constructed leads us to ask why it has been constructed in that way. We can then ask ourselves whether we shall permit it to remain that way or shall we challenge it. By critically exploring the way practice is constructed and how it is shaped by powerful discourses creates the opportunity to identify areas to change and rewrite the story (which is the reconstruction stage). The deconstruction of the narrative through critical reflection can unearth 'new ways to think about change and new ways to enhance change practices' (Morley, 2013:1). This is because 'critical reflection provides a way of "standing back" and seeing the issues from a different perspective' (Fook & Gardner, 2007:10).

The facilitator therefore needs to support the social worker during the process of deconstructing dominant ways of thinking. The skills of the facilitator are essential for encouraging the practitioner to see the self and their practice through an alternative lens. It is important to acknowledge that the narrator and facilitator may deconstruct differently 'resulting in contested meanings' (Riessman, 2001:704). However, being open to hearing alternative perspectives can make for rich dialogue and deeper insight for both parties.

So far, the social worker has related a situation from practice and with the support of the facilitator they have reflected upon the dominant ways of thinking that hinder and stifle practice; this leads to the next stage which is to reconstruct an alternative narrative. The reconstructing process requires the social worker to envision change and explore possible alternative relationships and amended power dynamics. This re-authoring/reconstruction of the narrative considers potential advancement through reframing the power relationships and identifies possibilities within procedures and practices. It is by exposing and acknowledging the discourses that constitute one's practice, that the social worker is afforded the opportunity to see alternatives and begin to explore how things can be constructed and perceived differently. The first case study presents an example of reconstructing an alternative narrative by a practitioner who works in adult safeguarding and the second is taken from a practitioner working within a third sector organisation.

Case Study 6.1

In this example the social worker draws upon dominant discourses of a lack of interagency collaboration and frustrations at the ever increasing amount of safeguarding referrals. The social worker's constructed narrative articulates 'other professionals' as 'disinterested' and 'reluctant to attend strategy meetings' and they frequently 'dump' the responsibility for adult safeguarding onto the social worker. The Care Act 2014 includes a statutory duty for local authorities to make enquiry and the social worker states 'so this is going to make it worse and we will have a flood of people ... they will make a referral and think they have done their bit ... you won't see them for dust'.

By reflecting on the discursive constructs the social worker identifies that she situates power with the referrer as they 'dump' and run. She situates herself as powerless as she has a duty to accept the case and struggles to engage other professionals in strategy planning. The practice of being the lead professional who has responsibility for safeguarding in a climate of inadequate community support services adds to her feeling of disempowerment and overwork. The facilitator assists her to explore the language she uses to characterise the behaviour of others, agency policy, principles of assessment, management of adult protection and the philosophy underpinning the changes made by the introduction of the Care Act 2014. This dialogue empowers the social worker to re-evaluate the power relations and to approach her dominant ways of thinking through a new lens. Rather than accept the inevitability of the situation, the shifting of perspective onto rebalancing power can aid the process of thinking about alternative strategies to practice. The deconstructing process assists the social worker to consider that she needs to be more explicit with multi-agency colleagues about expectations in relation to shared responsibility to risk and protection. The social worker can challenge the dump-and-run approach and consider ways to re-engage the referrer within the assessment process. The social worker may reconstruct the narrative to consider possibilities and collaborative strategies that reposition/rebalance power because she is empowered to challenge dominant ways of thinking and traditional responses to the situation.

Case Study 6.2

This case study example draws upon an experience the author and peers had while working alongside a colleague from a third sector agency (Larkins, Westwood, Berry & Stone, 2014). Our colleague (the narrator) works within a project that aims to raise the aspirations of looked-after young people and her concern was ensuring equality of opportunity and engagement. We used a template similar to Template 6.1 to note down phrases she used that related to the inclusion of young people and her narrative was audio recorded. In the deconstruction stage the narrator was encouraged to give reflective attention to phrases such as 'vote with their feet', 'ring I don't respond to email' and 'commitment to the bid'. The narrator was afforded a safe space to explore the discursive constructs that shaped her practice, which included the structure of the project and the relationships with 'others' involved. By exposing some of her beliefs about power, through dialogue she began to reconstruct alternative approaches to practice that encompassed working alongside looked-after young people, their carers and the local authority as corporate parents. There were many aspects outside the control and responsibility of her third sector agency but by critically reflecting upon the narrative it was possible to expose the potential discourses at play and to begin a refocusing of role, responsibility and other aspects of her practice with young people that were within her remit and that she had the power to change.

Tools

Template 6.1 has been designed to draw attention to the discourses at play by providing triggers to aid critical reflection and to stimulate thinking around ways to remove barriers and address challenges within practice. The template is a means to an end, not an end in itself, and therefore it will help you record words to stimulate thinking but will not provide the solutions. The content you decide to put into Template 6.1 must be given reflective consideration.

When deconstructing or reconstructing a narrative (spoken or textual) the questions in Template 6.1 are to be used as prompts as they suggest ways to deconstruct and reconstruct, and to begin critical reflection. It is not necessary to make an entry against each question.

Template 6.1 Advanced critical reflection through narrative (re)construction

Deconstructing the narrative	
What are the barriers/challenges identified?	
What words are used to describe the people?	
What words are used to describe the practices?	
Where does the social worker situate power?	
What are the factors that limit progress?	
Are there rules and practices that constrain/prohibit?	
How does the social worker's behaviour limit progress?	
How does the social worker's thinking limit progress?	
Other dominant thinking to note	
Other dominant thinking to note	
Other dominant thinking to note	
Reconstructing the narrative	
What alternative behaviour from the social worker can work to bringing about change?	
What alternative mindset/thinking by the social worker can work to bring about change?	
How can power be rebalanced?	
What theories of change can be drawn upon to challenge the dominant ways of thinking or bring about change?	
Other notes on reversing dominant assumptions	
Other notes on reversing dominant assumptions	
Other notes on reversing dominant assumptions	

Template inspired by Larkins et al. (2014)

Conclusion

The methodology of advanced critical reflection through narrative (re)construction involves speaking about a situation from practice, exploring the discursive constructs that the practitioner draws upon or which are at play, with a view to developing a more constructive narrative to inform future practice. Of course it is acknowledged that this methodology does not guarantee multi-agency cooperation in adult safeguarding (see Case Study 6.1 above) nor does it profess to resolve any of those situations upon which the practitioner critically reflects. What it does do is to facilitate a safe and supportive framework for practitioners to critically reflect upon discursive constructs that operate within an area of practice. Through this authoring process one may be able to identify those factors that limit and constrain, to explore whether they can envisage alternative approaches. Recognising the blocks within practice is an important step in being able to reconstruct alternative narratives and approaches to practice.

7

Supervision for Transformative Learning and the Development of Practice

Pam Snowball

Introduction

'Supervision is a process by which one worker is given responsibility by the organisation to work with another worker(s) in order to meet certain organisational, professional and personal objectives which together promote the best outcomes for service users' (Morrison, 2005:32). Social work is a profession that has to pay attention to the doing, thinking and feeling of its tasks. Supervision if delivered well is recognised as a valuable medium for developing and supporting social workers to be capable and confident professionals. 'Good quality, professional supervision recognises the interplay of cognition and feeling and the use of self in social work. 'Supervision is a professional conversation which should promote learning and reflective practice' (Carpenter, Webb, Bostock & Coomber, 2012:7).

This chapter speaks primarily to the social work practitioner or learner (the supervisee) to support them to get the best out of their supervision. However, because the principles and exercises are equally relevant to those who supervise, they too may find value in this chapter. Supervision theories and models are explored and inform the reflective exercises incorporated throughout this chapter. Tempting as it is to skip over them, these exercises are an important part of learning because they link theory and practice and can be used by supervisees and their supervisors, together or individually.

Key Points

- Relationships matter: for supervision to be really effective it should be carried out within the context of a purposeful and attuned professional relationship between the supervisor and supervisee.
- Supervision is part of the core business of social work and should be given due priority.
- Supervisors and supervisees have a shared responsibility to ensure that their supervision sessions include adequate time for reflection and to address the professional developmental needs of the supervisee.
- Effective supervision has a positive impact on outcomes for service users.

Significance for Social Work Practice

Supervision is part of the core business of social work and when things go wrong it is often the lack of quality or frequency of supervision that is highlighted as a contributory factor. As a direct response to concerns in the profession The Social Work Reform Board (SWRB) developed the Standards for Employers and Social Workers in England and Supervision Framework, which outlines good practice for social work employers (SWRB, 2012). These standards require employers to 'ensure that social workers have regular and appropriate social work supervision' (SWRB, 2012:6). The importance of supervision is also reinforced by the social work professional regulatory body, the Health and Care Professions Council (HCPC), who urge social workers to 'recognise the value of supervision' and develop their practice by using 'supervision to support and enhance the quality of social work practice' (HCPC, 2012b:12). This is because supervision is seen as a medium through which learning and reflective practice is promoted (Carpenter et al., 2012).

A comprehensive overview of research evidence into the effects of supervision conducted on behalf of The Social Care Institute for Excellence (SCIE) highlights the importance of providing opportunities for reflective supervision (Carpenter et al., 2012). Morrison (2005) locates supervision in the context of its impact on services users, staff, the organisation and also multi-agency partners. Because all of these stakeholders are beneficiaries, the importance of good supervision for safe and effective practice cannot be overstated.

Using in Practice

The case has been made that supervision is important for safe and effective practice and the subsections below address different aspects of supervision. The reflective prompts throughout encourage you to think about and address your supervisory experience to enable you to make the best use of supervision.

The Supervisory Relationship

This chapter is based on the premise that all good professional supervision is carried out within the context of a purposeful, effective relationship between the supervisee and their supervisor. Beddoe et al. (2014) highlight the significance of the supervisory relationship in terms of establishing 'a safe place to employ and strengthen the personal attributes of supervisees' which therefore positively impacts on practitioner well-being (Beddoe et al., 2014:119). This relationship is particularly important when the work gets messy and stressful and the supervisee is in need of someone to help contain their anxiety and boost their emotional resilience to face the difficulties of the work. Research by Manthorpe et al. (2015) suggests that NQSWs 'value their supervisory encounters [and] the ways in which supervision seems to enhance engagement with their work' (Manthorpe, Moriarty, Hussein, Stevens & Sharpe, 2015:65). However, the symbiotic relationship between the supervisor and the supervisee can be the factor that makes supervision successful or not. As in all relationships, this is a two-way process and the supervisee has as much responsibility as the supervisor to work on this relationship and to address difficulties.

The foundation of a professional purposeful relationship relies upon the ability of both parties to have open and honest discussions about any concerns they have. For this to be effective they need to be able to trust each other and to have mutual respect for the strengths they each bring to supervision and to be able to acknowledge the limits of their expertise. It is important to clarify expectations of supervision and to pay attention to the process between the supervisor and supervisee. Providing a safe space within supervision enables the supervisee to begin to trust the supervisor and to recognise the value of reflective discussion.

- What aspects of your supervisory relationship do you most value?
- What aspects of your supervisory relationship do you least value?
- What three positive changes in your supervisory relationship would you like to make?
- What can you do to bring about these changes?
- Who or what can help you?
- What would be different about your supervisory relationship if these changes were achieved?
- What would you be doing differently in supervision?
- What would your supervisor be doing differently?

The priority that the supervisor gives to supervision is demonstrated by the attention they give to providing a safe and supportive environment. The supervisor has a responsibility to act as a role model and to behave in a manner that is conducive to building trust. For example, supervisees will make negative assumptions about the importance their supervisor gives to them and their work if the supervisor does not give much eye-contact and spends most of the supervision behind their desk typing up a record of the session. It is difficult for supervisees to feel safe in opening up about their concerns if the supervisor does not provide a safe haven for such discussions to take place. Attention should be paid to practical considerations, such as the best available room, the seating arrangements, the management of potential interruptions, and the use of mobile phones.

Supervision History

Individuals do not approach a supervision session in an emotionally neutral way and one of the biggest influences on your current experiences is your previous experience of supervision. With this in mind Morrison (2005) advocates reflecting upon your previous supervision experiences. Template 7.1 supports you in considering your supervision history and encourages you to share your reflections with your current supervisor/supervisee.

Template 7.1 Supervision history

Thinking about your experiences, what was it about the style of supervision that you found most helpful and supportive?
How did your responses/behaviour contribute?
What was it about the supervisor's style that you found least helpful?
How did your responses/behaviour contribute?
What learning do you take from this reflection, which may be relevant to your current supervisory relationship?
What action are you going to take?

A manager who completed this exercise on one of my training courses recently said that completing a supervision history prompted her to question the way she thought about the supervision she facilitated and how she allowed workers to easily postpone or re-arrange supervision. On reflection she suspected that her own supervisors in the past had not attributed much value to supervision sessions and she had unwittingly carried this practice on into her current delivery of supervision sessions.

Current practice is influenced by past experiences and, through reflection and overt acknowledgement, practitioners can ensure that they are not pre-determined by their past.

Supervisee's Rights and Responsibilities

Supervision does not happen in a vacuum and it is important to consider the organisational context within which supervision occurs and the agency's definition of supervision. This is particularly important when a supervisee or supervisor feels that supervision is not living up to their expectations. The questions within Template 7.2 focus attention on the supervisee's rights and responsibilities in relation to supervision.

Template 7.2 Supervisee's rights and responsibilities

Have you read your agency's supervision policy?
How does it define supervision: its content, frequency and the rights and responsibilities of supervisors and supervisees?
Does it match your definition and expectations for supervision?
What will do you differently as a result of having a better understanding of the meaning of supervision?
What should you discuss with your supervisor?
How are you going to approach your supervision differently now?

From doing this exercise you may have considered what your rights are to have supervision and what your responsibility is within the supervisory relationship. The distinction between rights and responsibilities can be very subtle but both are important and examples of each are set out in the checklist below. The key value of this list is to promote a professional discussion between supervisor and supervisee and to clarify expectations for both parties, which could form the basis of a supervision contract (covered later in the chapter). There may be more that you want to add to this supervisees rights and responsibilities checklist which has been adapted from Morrison 2005.

Supervisee's Rights and Responsibilities Checklist (adapted from Morrison 2005)

- To accept the organisation's mandate to be supervised and accountable for your practice.
- To negotiate a supervisory contract compatible with the organisation's supervision policy.
- To attend regularly and promptly and endeavour to minimise disruptions.
- To agree an agenda and actively participate.
- To be open and share information.
- To promote anti-oppressive practice.
- To have permission to express feelings and to be listened to.
- To actively pursue continual professional development.

- To give and accept constructive feedback and challenges.
- To be willing to learn from mistakes and know that is it acceptable to admit that you may have 'got it wrong'.
- To have experience, skills and knowledge affirmed.
- To reflect, consider and explore options.

As a supervisee how clear are you about the above? Are there parts of this list that need to be discussed and made more explicit in your supervision sessions?

The Supervision Contract

The main reason to agree a supervision contract is to clarify roles and expectations and expose assumptions. Exploring these areas can pre-empt misunderstandings and identify remedial processes should difficulties be encountered in the future. The co-construction of the contract is an important stage in the development of a trusting and respectful relationship between supervisor and supervisee.

Template 7.3 provides the content for a supervision contract and all aspects must be discussed by the supervisor and supervisee. It is also important to take into consideration existing supervision policies and requirements.

Template 7.3 Supervision contract

Names of supervisee and supervisor	
Organisation's expectations such as frequency and length of sessions	
How we will manage cancellations and re-arrangement of sessions	
Location and other practical considerations. E.g. how we will manage interruptions	
Responsibility for recording and storing of supervision records	
How will the agenda for each session be agreed?	
What I want from you as my supervisor	
What I will contribute as a supervisee to ensure this happens	

(Continued)

Template 7.3 *(Continued)*

What I want from you as a supervisee	
What I will contribute as a supervisor to ensure this happens	
Permissions that have been agreed. E.g. it is ok for the supervisee to say they are stuck and for the supervisor to say they do not know.	
What we will do if problems arise in our working together.	

This template has been adapted from Morrison (2005)

The Supervision Agenda

The agenda for supervision ought to be based upon the purpose and principles of supervision and should include all that needs to be covered in the supervision session. There are many different models of supervision we can draw upon, but I find it helpful to think of supervision as covering four main domains: administration and the management of performance, professional development, reflection on practice and offering personal support. The **administrative function** provides both supervisor and supervisee with a mandate to ensure that agency processes and procedures are appropriately implemented and recorded. **Professional development** is an important aspect of supervision where learning opportunities are identified to provide continual learning and development. **Reflection** is a central feature of social work practice and it is through reflection that the supervisee will develop their own problem solving skills. Given the emotive and often distressing nature of social work it is not surprising that it can have an emotional impact on the practitioner and therefore **personal support** is important. Only by bringing into awareness the personal emotional impact of the work can a practitioner be supported to address it.

From my experience of discussing the priorities given to each of these elements, practitioners will often state that their supervision sessions focus on the administrative function. Indeed, research conducted by Jack and Donnellan (2010) found that often managers were perceived by NQSWs to be more concerned with completing tasks on time than to 'support them in the way that they thought was warranted' (Jack & Donnellan, 2010:312). It is easy to see why this may be the case when busy managers and practitioners meet within tight time limits. The work that, quite correctly, may exercise their minds the most are the situations that are perceived as the most risky. Supervisors want reassurance that the correct procedures have been followed, the risks have been addressed and supervisees want to be reassured that their practice is safe and correct. No one goes into supervision in a neutral state of mind and anxiety can influence our discussions in subtle and significant ways. It is important to attend to the administrative aspects within supervision but reflection, support and development must not be overlooked.

Regardless of the agenda item being covered in supervision, engaging in reflective practice is essential to enable you to discuss your experiences within your case work, voice your concerns, express your developmental needs and negotiate appropriate supportive mechanisms. In the remainder of this chapter, prominence is given to reflection within supervision as I encourage you to reflect on, and for supervision to support you to get the best out of, your supervision relationship and supervision experience.

A suggested supervision agenda is provided as Template 7.4 and can be used to prompt discussion between supervisor and supervisee. It should not be used as a tick box exercise, which mitigates against the promotion of reflective supervision. It should be located in your organisation's supervision policy and pay attention to the agenda items your organisation requires you to address in supervision. Please use the suggestions in Template 7.4 as applicable to your situation with your organisation or learning provider.

Template 7.4 Supervision agenda

Agree the agenda for today's supervision meeting	
Review work via discussion, reports and observation	
Agree and review action plans	
Identify skills and knowledge development and gaps to address	
Reflect upon your experiences and feelings about your work	
Identify and discuss an area of your work that went well since the last supervision session	

This template has been adapted from Morrison (2005)

Reflective Supervision

Wonnacott (2012) carried out very interesting research into how supervision styles affect outcomes for children and families where there were child protection concerns. This was a small-scale piece of research which identified three different supervision styles: active intrusive; passive and active reflective. The active reflective style appeared to have the most positive influence on outcomes for service users and was the style that most research participants would want to emulate. This style is collaborative, reflective and challenging. It also enables the supervisor to have an accurate understanding of the worker's capabilities and focuses on tasks and processes while paying attention to the emotional impact of the work and the stage of development of the worker.

Morrison (2005) identified key links between supervision, good practice and outcomes which are helpful headings to explore within a reflective supervisory relationship, such as role clarity, emotional intelligence, observation and assessment of the worker's capabilities and appropriate partnership and power.

Role Clarity

To be an effective social worker and develop your professional self, practitioners need to be clear about their role. This is particularly useful when they may be overwhelmed by certain aspects of their job or feel that they are floundering. It is worth re-visiting the job description and career development goals and development plans.

> *Do you understand what is expected of you within your role?*
>
> *Can you identify gaps in your knowledge and skills that need to be addressed?*
>
> *If you are unclear about your role in relation to the work you are doing, it is important to discuss this in supervision, otherwise your ability to work well, particularly in difficult situations, will be compromised.*

Supervisors are in an excellent position to be able to help workers achieve role clarity, which has an importance influence on how confident and secure they feel as a professional social worker.

Emotional Intelligence

Emotional intelligence is explored fully in Chapter 3 but the reader is reminded to consider both the intra and interpersonal aspects of emotional competence within the supervision relationship. Template 7.5 encourages reflection on emotional intelligence in relation to supervision. It draws attention to the emotions at play for both parties within the supervisory relationship.

Template 7.5 Emotional intelligence within the supervision relationship

Consider how often you check into how you are feeling before you begin a supervision session.
What is your emotional state before, during and after supervision?
Do you know what may be affecting your emotional state?
How do your emotions impact (both positively and negatively) on the supervision experience?
How do you/or could you manage your interactions?
What do you do to tune into the emotional state of your supervisor/supervisees during the supervision session?
What will you do differently in your supervision sessions as a result of identifying your emotional state?

Observation and Assessment of the Worker's Capabilities

The profession is very much based on the assumption that social workers are continually learning but it is important that practitioners feel that carrying out their professional duties and developing their professional self is within their grasp. Being able to recognise their skills and knowledge and ask for support when they need it is indicative of their development towards a mature and balanced professional.

There is value in observing practitioners for assessment and performance management yet it is important to remember that social workers may not be so comfortable with their live practice being observed and assessed. However, framed within a trusting relationship, with the feedback presented clearly and sensitively, this can be a very powerful learning medium. The supervisor and supervisee can negotiate what aspects of practice are to be observed and make arrangements for the facilitation of learning from feedback from the observer and also service users. It is through constructive and specific feedback that individuals can identify where and how to make changes.

Supervision is an excellent arena for helping to identify the skills and knowledge that practitioners are not consciously aware of through reflection and analysis. This is particularly useful in developing practitioner skills, emotional intelligence and resilience.

Appropriate Partnership and Power

In theory, supervision should provide a safe haven for supervisees to discuss their doubts and worries to enable them to bring into awareness feelings and thoughts that may hitherto have remained hidden. A trusting and predictable relationship is key to good supervision. We know that in order to practise safely in an emotive environment social workers need to feel some of the attunement that good practitioners provide to service users. Achieving appropriate partnership and purposeful power relationships in supervision is the very bedrock of good practice. Remember that it is your responsibility to consider what you want to get from supervision and to take the steps to improve the supervisory experience. The four questions in Template 7.6 encourage you to consider partnership and power at play within supervision. The aim of the questions is to stimulate honest reflection with a view to acknowledging things which go well and identifying aspects which require improvement and change.

Template 7.6 Partnership and power in supervision

How do you discuss power/authority in your relationship with your supervisor/supervisee?	
As a supervisee what power and authority do you consider your supervisor holds?	
As a supervisor how do you ensure that power and authority is openly addressed in your supervision sessions?	
Power and authority are important features in relationships with service users. What learning might you take from your supervisory relationship into your practice with service users?	

Supervisees may feel that supervision is something that is done to them but for supervision to be effective Hawkins and Shohet (2007) acknowledge that the stage of the social worker in their career can have an influence on the type of supervision style that is most appropriate for the individual worker, with newly qualified workers requiring a more directive approach on occasions.

Tony Morrison is well known and respected for his writings about supervision for social work practice. He was a key writer in the development of supervision standards published by the Children's Workforce Development Council and has written numerous books and articles on supervision (some of which have been used within this chapter). I have introduced you to Tony Morrison's '4×4×4 model' of supervision, as it is a very useful model that draws together the crucial factors of supervision and emphasises the need to remind ourselves that for supervision to be effective it has to have an impact on social work practice. The '4×4×4 model' identifies 4 stakeholders affected by supervision: service users, social workers, the organisation and partner agencies. He identifies 4 functions of supervision outlined above: the administrative function, professional development, reflection and personal support. I have paid particular attention to the features of the model that can be implemented practically by supervisors and supervisees to develop reflective practice and improve the effectiveness of their supervision experience.

The final 4 in this model refers to the process of supervision and is based on Kolb's learning cycle which places prominence on the notion that adults learn best by paying attention to their experiences, reflecting on their thoughts and feelings, and using formal knowledge and experimentation or action (Kolb, 1984). A good quality, well-rounded learning experience will pay attention to all parts of the learning cycle but we all have a tendency to sit more naturally in one part of the cycle. By being very aware of our preferences we can identify how we learn best and also the areas we tend to neglect and need to give more attention to in order to develop our learning. Our preferences can change over time according to the context within which we work and the preferred styles of the people we work with. Sometimes conflict between colleagues can be due to very different styles of learning. A supervisor with an activist style may struggle to understand why a very reflective worker doesn't 'just get on with it!' Understanding how we best learn and our different styles can be an important factor in finding the best ways of working together in supervision. The quality of learning is enhanced by understanding our own preferred ways of learning and also by stretching ourselves intellectually to embrace the preferences of others.

Morrison's model draws heavily on Kolb's learning cycle to explore the process by which both parties can assess the situation faced by the worker and reflect upon the feelings and thoughts raised by the experience, consider what theory and research can be usefully drawn upon and how they can move forward. So the supervision cycle consists of experience, reflection, analysis and action (Kolb, 1984).

It is important that attention is given to the reflective and theoretical part of the process, rather than jumping straight from experience to action and the next steps, particularly where there is no obvious correct action to take. Where there is an immediate, identified risk that requires decisive action, the time for reflection may be afforded later. But much of the more complex work we do does not have simple solutions. Grint (2008) identified problems that do not have straightforward solutions, or a necessarily right or wrong answer, as 'wicked problems' and this has relevance to social work practice.

> With wicked problems you need to get a really good look at what you are dealing with. That means collaboration and asking the right questions of the right people. (Baim & Morrison, 2011:316)

Reflective questioning can aid identification of the problem and help to co-construct a good understanding of the pertinent information and a potential way forward. The reflective questions within Template 7.7 (adapted from Morrison 2005) provide a structure to facilitate reflective conversations in supervision.

Template 7.7 Reflective questions for supervision

➢ List 3 assumptions you, the practitioner, brought with you into this case/session?	
➢ How do you define your role in relation to this service user and/or family?	
➢ What does the service user think is your role?	

➢ What were your aims for the session/this piece of work?	
➢ What was achieved?	
➢ What wasn't achieved?	
➢ What previous work, skills and knowledge are relevant?	
➢ Who/What does this service user remind you of?	
➢ What was most or least uncomfortable for you and when?	
➢ What feelings are you left with?	

Engaging in dialogue during a supervisory session can assist you to explore an area of practice in depth. Another useful area of focus during supervision is those situations which cause anxiety. Seigel (2007) demonstrates very clearly how the brain responds to feelings of perceived threat or stress by relying on the primitive part of the brain, the limbic system, which activates our fight, freeze, flight responses and jumps quickly into action, overpowering our thinking part of the brain: the cortex. When these responses are activated we cannot use our cortex to reflect on our thoughts and feelings and this results in not being able to think straight and not being able to engage in constructive and reflective dialogue in supervision. With this in mind, Template 7.8 can be used when you have high levels of anxiety which may be impeding your ability to engage in reflective dialogue in supervision.

Template 7.8 Addressing anxieties in supervision

What is it about practice that activates your fight, freeze, flight responses and overpowers your thinking?	
What is it about supervision that activates your fight, freeze, flight responses and overpowers your thinking?	
What are the barriers to raising these issues in supervision?	
What would help you to discuss these issues with your supervisor?	
What have you learnt about yourself from reflecting on the above questions?	

Peer and Group Supervision

While the model of supervision discussed in this chapter has focused on one-to-one supervision, all the above principles can be applied to group supervision. The reflective questions can be used as discussion prompts and peer group supervision can be an excellent complement to the more formal one-to-one sessions. Social work has an aural tradition and most social workers value the opportunity to discuss complex work with trusted colleagues. Beddoe et al. (2014) discovered that 'a pro-resilient organisation facilitates ongoing learning and mentoring opportunities, collegial support and reflective practice' (Beddoe et al., 2014:116).

Case Study 7.1

Emma is a newly qualified social worker in a busy city centre children's initial referral and assessment team. She is six months into her first job as a qualified worker. She completed her final placement as part of her Social Work degree on a similar team in the same local authority in the city suburbs, which she enjoyed immensely and felt that she had an excellent relationship with her practice educator.

Emma is disappointed that her relationship with her current supervisor, Jill, does not live up to her expectations. She feels that Jill does not understand her and supervision sessions are often rushed and task focused. Emma often leaves supervision sessions feeling more overwhelmed than when she went in. She does not like to refuse to do anything Jill asks of her and feels anxious when she does not understand the tasks she has been asked to undertake. Emma worries that she is in danger of not achieving the standards Jill expects by the end of her first year and so she wants to make a good impression in supervision.

Emma realises that she had different expectations for supervision than her supervisor and that some of the reasons for this may be to do with the change from being a student on placement to a qualified social worker. In order to stem her feelings of being overwhelmed and achieve more control in her supervision sessions Emma requested that they discuss the rights and responsibility checklist (see above). This gave them the opportunity to discuss her own and her supervisor's rights and responsibilities in supervision. From this discussion and the clarity they achieved, the supervision sessions became better planned, more structured and less rushed.

Emma also requested that they discuss her supervision history. This enabled Emma to first reflect on the attributes she had valued in her previous supervisor.

▶

> She recognised that her practice educator had, quite rightly, focused on the supportive, developmental functions of supervision. Through an open discussion with her supervisor she acknowledged the importance of attending to tasks but was also able to express her need for more overt supportive and developmental time in supervision rather than case management dominating the agenda. Jill was surprised that Emma was feeling overwhelmed and had been pleased with the progress that Emma was making but recognised that she did not always express positive feedback in a manner that was specific and obvious to Emma. The discussion of both the supervisee's rights and responsibilities and supervision history (see above) allowed Emma and Jill to discuss their expectations and explore difficulties in a non-threatening manner.

Conclusion

Too often supervisors and supervisees find supervision difficult but struggle to find ways of addressing the problems for fear of offending each other. Supervisees tell me that they do not want to express their dissatisfaction to their supervisor for fear of being seen as incapable. This is worrying, given that supervision should be a place where workers feel safe enough to express their doubts and emotions. Equally, supervisors sometimes lack the confidence to try different ways to address their concerns about their supervisee's practice and can become stuck in a cycle of despondency about their supervisee's development. It is interesting that as practitioners we have difficult conversations with service users on a daily basis and often tell people things that they do not want to hear, yet we struggle to use those same skills to address difficulties in supervision. For supervision to be effective, these difficulties have to be addressed and in doing so there are opportunities for the relationship between supervisee and supervisor, the very bedrock on which good supervision is based, to grow and strengthen.

The tools discussed above provide less threatening and professional ways of addressing difficulties in the supervisory process and can be suggested by either parties.

If you are a practitioner reflecting on whether you should address your supervisory needs with your supervisor, it is worth reminding yourself that you have a professional responsibility to get the very best out of your supervision. Indeed as Beddoe et al. (2014) discovered 'self-defined, resilient practitioners were very active in taking responsibility for their own well-being' (Beddoe et al., 2014:125).

8
Coaching for Social Workers

Bobby Chatterjee

Introduction

Coaching can be described as a process of asking a series of questions in a non-judgemental manner in order to work through and explore different perspectives and discover one or more options for the way forward. It could also be described as a conversation with a purpose. It is a forward-looking approach to facilitating a person's thinking in order to help them to move forward and create change.

It is common practice in business and sport to procure the services of a professional coach for significant problem solving, career management, confidence-building, personal brand management and when making transitions to new levels or sectors. That said, it is a highly pragmatic and valuable tool, whether or not you are able to secure the services of a coach.

For the purposes of this chapter, there are two methods to coaching. First, the principles discussed here can also be used with a colleague willing to be your coaching partner, where you offer each other the opportunity to be coached. Second, the same principles can be applied to improve your self-coaching ability. Self-coaching means:

- To provide yourself with questions and challenges about the current situation or aim.
- To understand what is really causing your emotional reaction or feeling of being stuck.
- To find new and alternative solutions to problems and conflicts.

Coaching utilises and explores the resourcefulness of the whole human being to benefit the individual being coached (the coachee) and the organisation they work for. Within the field of social work, coaching can also be a very powerful way to unlock solutions and ideas during direct work with service users, their families and communities.

As a skill, and indeed a profession for some, coaching is highly unusual in that the coach does not necessarily have to be an expert in the topic area being focused upon. This allows the coach to be entirely on the coachee's agenda, without judgement or personal agenda, and to demonstrate a genuine curiosity and encouragement towards the coachee achieving their stated goals and intentions. Therefore, for self-coaching or working with a coaching partner, there should be no barrier to being able to coach; all that is needed is a genuine interest and good quality searching questions. As with any skill, our ability to coach will naturally improve over time once we see the effectiveness of the intervention for ourselves. Once coaching/self-coaching becomes a habit, coaching will become very straightforward and a useful method for problem-solving.

It is important to clarify what coaching is not, to avoid any misunderstanding. When asked to define 'coaching', many people who firmly believe they are good coaches are, in actual fact, unable to define coaching correctly, often suggesting that it is 'advising and guiding' or 'offering your views to reach solutions'. These two suggestions are more akin to the skill of mentoring which is about sharing your experience, knowledge and insight to help and advise someone, usually less experienced or more junior than you. While mentoring is also a very useful skill, this chapter focuses on coaching, as it can be done without having to find a suitable mentor who has experience of the situation you may wish to discuss. Reflecting on your practice within your formal or informal supervision sessions may span across both coaching and mentoring. Outside of these opportunities, self-coaching can be highly valuable because it can develop resilience and enable the generation of solutions to problems in a structured manner. All of the exercises within the chapter can be used in either partner coaching or self-coaching.

Key Points

Within coaching, the person who is being coached is called the coachee. A core assumption when commencing any coaching conversation is that, 'the coachee is capable of much better results than they are currently generating' (Starr, 2008:48). Therefore, for self-coaching, the person coaching themselves must believe that there is a way forward and one or more options, even if none are known at the start. By working through a given situation by asking yourself questions, it effectively holds a mirror up by playing back your words, your emotions and your struggles, while asking powerful questions to both unlock any blockage in your thinking and generate a commitment to take action in moving forward. Think of coaching like completing a jigsaw. The coachee has expressed a wish to complete the jigsaw but doesn't yet know quite what the picture looks like. The coach's role is to assist the coachee to find the right pieces and to clarify what the picture is of.

Significance for Social Work Practice

Social workers and student social workers will encounter the full range of human emotions in their work and so the ability to self-coach could prove very valuable indeed for generating faster resolutions to problems and conflicts both within oneself and with others.

As a social worker or student social worker, coaching is a great way to understand and work with your emotional reactions (see also Chapter 3 on Emotional Intelligence). 'Change the way you think and this, in turn, will change the way you feel. Understanding your view of events provides insight into why you feel and act in the ways that you do. Armed with this knowledge, you can then decide if you want to change this viewpoint in favour of one likely to bring you better results' (Neenan & Dryden, 2008: ix). Furthermore, the ability to reflect and ask powerful non-judgemental coaching questions is a great skill for helping service users.

Using in Practice

To establish what is underlying your current emotions in a particular situation, there are three key emotional insight questions to ask yourself:

1. What is the emotion I am feeling? (Emotional Vocabulary and Template 8.3)

Be more descriptive than with general emotions like 'happy' and 'sad'.

2. Why am I feeling or experiencing this emotion?

   – Is it because of the actual situation or circumstances (effectively the 'facts of the case') or

   – Is it because of my internal interpretation of what that situation means? This can, for example, be the self-talking commentary or perspective on what that means when we extrapolate what actually did happen or what we believe has happened and what that means for us, moving forward.

3. What does that insight mean for me?

Having established which of the options is at the root of the emotion or interpretation, the next step is to ask yourself some powerful questions to generate a full understanding of the situation and your aim(s) within it. If you consider the way a problem-solving conversation typically takes place, there are sequentially questions for different purposes. Starr (2008) draws attention to the need to gather information and focus on the situation with a view to generating an understanding upon which the options are considered. Following logical steps in this way can help you to explore alternatives and Template 8.1 offers structure to support this process. Begin by reflecting upon a difficult situation that you have encountered and take your time to answer each step as a coaching scenario. Template 8.1 guides you through the difficult situations and offers examples of powerful questions.

Template 8.1 Difficult situations and powerful questions

Gather a general overview – *What happened with the service user in the last conversation?*	
Gather the specific details – *What did he actually say or do? Which parts of his/her behaviour caused me to react emotionally, or to feel some sort of emotion now?*	
Anchor attention to the present moment – *What does that mean for me now?*	

(*Continued*)

Template 8.1 (*Continued*)

Understand your own perspective and the perspective of the other person – *How sure am I that I fully understood his perspective without any misunderstandings or assumptions? What do I believe are his reasons for his behaviour and his actions? What might he have been feeling during that conversation? Could he have misunderstood my intentions?*	
Create options – *What can I do about this to move things forward? What else can I do?*	
Move towards a conclusion – *What are my thoughts about this situation now? What is the most important point to focus on?*	
Check commitment to taking action – *Which of the options that I have generated am I committed to take? When will I take this action? What are the consequences if I don't take any action now? How will I overcome any barriers to achieving this outcome?*	

When coaching with your coaching partner, the coach can use the above headings to frame the questions and help the coachee to reflect, analyse, construct options and commit to action.

You can also follow the structure of the ACORN model to ask questions within each of the sections (see Figure 8.1 and Template 8.2).

Within coaching, the supervisee may at times feel they are stuck and perceive there to be barriers blocking the way. The metaphor for this situation is of being on a journey and then suddenly feeling unable to continue due to at least one roadblock ahead. Once we start to doubt our ability to see a clear way around the roadblock, we may find ourselves justifying that there is no point in trying or that perhaps we are just not able to complete our journey today – that is, before we establish whether any of that is true. These are limiting beliefs in self-coaching and coaching relationships need to be identified and reframed quickly to avoid any unhelpful, negative habits being formed over time which may derail our progress from within. A prudent commitment you could give yourself through coaching is the challenge to limit any limiting beliefs and to only introduce a new habit where it is positive.

Limiting beliefs are effectively distorted thinking, something that can happen to anyone relatively easily and often quite inadvertently at first. It classically happens in a number of ways, four of which are: magnification/minimisation; personalisation; 'shoulds' and 'musts'; and overgeneralisation (Neenan & Dryden, 2008:5) and are described below.

Magnification/minimisation refers to the loss of a sense of proportion where a person minimises their focus on the positives of a situation, however notable, choosing instead to magnify and exaggerate the negatives. **Personalisation** is an attempt to blame oneself for events outside of our control, for example, that our action (or indeed inaction) 'caused' someone to take the action they took. It implies that each person does not make their own choices and is entirely open to the influence of someone else. **Shoulds and musts** refer to the self-imposed rigid rules, boundaries and expectations we put on ourselves and others. If we fail to live up to those rules, we can feel inadequate and the longer this continues, the less able we are to see that we are equally able to choose a more flexible approach as our rigid version. **Over-generalisation** happens when we generalise one particular situation or event to all that may happen in the future, even if it is not actually relevant to do so. It implies that we believe we are not in conscious control of what happens in the future and that we can assume that, as this has happened once, it will undoubtedly occur again and we will not be any better equipped to handle it in the future.

It is important to recognise a distorted thought in yourself so that the distorted view does not become a pattern of behaviour which will over time become a pattern of self-expectation and reactions. To remove these limiting beliefs we should challenge ourselves as to whether we have blown the situation, or what we think of the situation, out of proportion. Take notice of your words to describe this part. If they include conclusive words such as always, never, couldn't, wouldn't, worst then ask yourself how do I know that for sure? Is there even a one per cent chance that this statement could not be completely true? This allows you to see that there is always a possibility that there is another answer or a different way of perceiving a situation.

Case Study 8.1: **(Self-coaching)**

Jo was a student social worker. She had specifically requested a placement in a Domestic Violence unit. After several attempted conversations, she tried a self-coaching approach to explore why she was having so much difficulty when

➤

she tried to speak to Anna, a service user. Anna presented as a highly anxious individual, wrestling with the decision to remain in the support of the unit rather than to return home to a periodic domestic violence situation with her husband. Despite really wanting to support Anna, Jo was increasingly feeling that she was perhaps being too pushy with her, and too directive towards the decisions that she believed she should make to change her life for the better.

Asking herself the three Emotional Insight questions (see Using in Practice, above) led to a realisation that her initial assumption of a personality clash was actually a deeper frustration in not having yet been able to 'connect' with Anna to allow her to truly support her. This understanding led to far more productive next steps, as the next time Jo spoke to Anna she opened up about not feeling connected and her hope that Anna did not misinterpret the lack of connection for a lack of support or care. That positive self-disclosure allowed their relationship to move on to a much better footing from then on.

Case Study 8.2: **(Coaching Partner)**

David was a qualified social worker. He asked his partner coach to provide some coaching for a situation with Joanna, a six-year-old girl he was working with. Joanna's mother, a single unemployed parent, was struggling financially to keep them both fed and David had noticed that Joanna was losing weight over a period of months. He was aware of the available procedures and would follow them but having grown very fond of Joanna, he realised he was potentially overstepping boundaries by regularly taking them both food.

His partner coach helped him to explore why he felt a significant connection in this situation. Together they explored the very real likelihood that many of the service users he encountered would 'bond' with him as he was an approachable, helpful person and they were often quite vulnerable. They explored whether he reacted in the same way to all different types of vulnerability and he reflected that he did not. His coach non-judgementally asked how he could ensure that he maintained the balance of behaving professionally throughout, but with sufficient support and warmth to ensure they felt able to open up to him in difficult circumstances. His coach then asked a number of insightful questions once they started exploring options to take him forward, for example: 'Thinking about any occasions where you felt you could potentially become more personally involved with the service user and their family, what were the signs that it may turn out that way?' David realised that, with his own background in a low-income family, he had a higher propensity to become more personally involved in those situations. His coach asked him further questions to help him evaluate the consequences of continuing that behaviour without changing. David was very clear that he had to change this behaviour and would also raise it in his next supervision.

David concluded that he now understood what was at the root of his different behaviour and generated two points to keep himself on track. First, he would evaluate the extent to which he had not become more personally involved through self-coaching, each time he was supporting a service user in a similar situation. Second, he would revisit all of the procedures for dealing with such situations and ensure that he was fully familiar with what he should and should not do. He was glad of the coaching conversation as he had not been able to understand why he got into that situation previously and felt confident that he would not find himself in the same dilemma in the future.

The ACORN Model

The ACORN acronym and model offers a clear structure with which to work through a particular situation within a coaching context. The ACORN model (see Figure 8.1) provides a visual illustration of the five domains for consideration within coaching. These domains are further broken down with reflective questions detailed within Template 8.2.

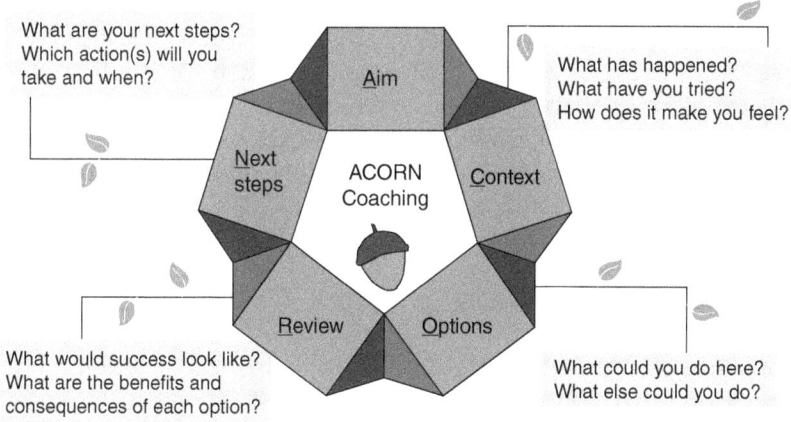

Figure 8.1 ACORN model

Template 8.2 ACORN coaching

A	Aim What is the aim for the coaching? Overall what would you like to achieve? What is this conversation about?	
C	Context What is the situation so far? What has happened? What have you already tried and what was the outcome? How is this situation making you feel and why? Consider what you know for sure during the recap of the situation.	
O	Options What options or actions could take this situation forward? What else? Initially don't worry if a particular option seems unrealistic as it is important not to discount options too early. Keep an open mind as you consider what could be done.	
R	Review What are the pros and cons of each action to evaluate them? How committed are you to take the action(s) most likely to move you forward on a scale of 1–10 where 1 is low and 10 is high? If lower than a score of 8, what would make your commitment higher? This may signify that there is something further to explore in either the Context (C) or further evaluation of consequences in Review (R).	
N	Next steps What are your next steps? Which action(s) will you take and when?	

It is perfectly normal as the coachee to move both forwards and backwards between the sections, particularly when explaining the situation in supervision or to your partner coach for the first time. The situation becomes very real when it is voiced, for example you may have started to discuss Options (O) then realised there is another important point to mention in the Context (C) section and moved back to that before resuming Options (O).

Emotional Vocabulary

The aim of Template 8.3 below is to help you to explore the emotion(s) that you are feeling about a particular situation. Often in conversation, we tend to use very simplistic labels to describe how we are feeling, such as happy and sad. By using a wide range of emotional descriptor words in your vocabulary, you become more discerning with your description. This, in turn, allows you (or your coaching partner) to explore where that particular emotion stems from and to consider the intensity of that emotion (intense, average, light). The descriptors coupled with the perception of intensity will also help you to develop your emotional intelligence.

The definitions of the words are your definitions of the words. They are simply an aid to your description and exploration and are not an exhaustive list. Some descriptors have natural opposites and others not. If you feel that any core descriptors are missing, these can be added in the blank spaces in the grid. Both positive and negative emotion descriptors are included as both provide useful information.

The words included in Template 8.3 may be particularly useful during the Context (C) section of ACORN, when describing how you feel about this situation or in a supervision discussion. Ask yourself why you have chosen that word and if that descriptor is really what you mean and feel.

The next step is to consider whether this emotional descriptor is the one you want to feel about this situation. For example, 'I felt really undermined by her comments but I can see now that I want to feel more comfortable when I receive feedback.' Then once into the Options (O) coaching section, explore how you could move towards that more positive feeling. It is important to be clear with yourself about the emotion that you wish to feel instead, so as to focus your mind on what you want. A person cannot feel two opposing emotions at the same time. For example, you cannot be very tense and laugh at the same time.

If you have previous experience of a similar situation where you felt more positive, use the coaching questions to consider what is different in this situation. Contrasting a current situation where an intense negative emotion is being described with a similar situation which had a positive emotion may provide additional insight. Template 8.3 only lists 40 emotions but it provides an example of how an emotional vocabulary can be developed. Please add your own words to the emotional vocabulary bank. The Template guides you through naming and reflecting upon your emotions and, where relevant, considering moving towards a more desired state.

Template 8.3 Emotional vocabulary

Happy	Sad	Proud	Ashamed	Conflicted
Comfortable	Miserable	Surprised	Shocked	Devastated
Optimistic	Pessimistic	Calm	Angry	Inadequate
Motivated	Demotivated	Sceptical	Suspicious	Confused
Empowered	Undermined	Threatened	Worried	Fearful
Sociable	Withdrawn	Resentful	Irritated	Stressed
Confident	Anxious	Accepted	Frustrated	Uncertain
Excited	Apprehensive	Delighted	Disappointed	Exhausted

Begin by circling one or more words (you may add your own) and then decide the intensity of each emotion. By the side of the word write I for intense, A for average or L for light intensity of emotion.

Where does that emotion(s) come from and what does it mean to you?

An alternative emotion that I would like to feel is?

Ways that I can move towards that more positive feeling:

Visualisation

Visualisation is a highly effective tool once you have decided on a goal but have not yet achieved it. The aim of the exercise is to consider in great detail the ideal resolution to your situation or goal. Capture your goal in the fullest detail possible under each of the five senses as shown in the grid below. The important point is to write in completing now rather than writing in the future tense, as if you had leapt forward in time and were looking at the success you are having in that moment. For example, 'I regularly chair a multi-agency meeting' rather than 'I will have chaired a multi-agency meeting.'

The unconscious mind is unable to distinguish between actual fact and aspirations when created in the present tense because the only input it has is from your conscious mind. Therefore, creating your intended outcome in the fullest detail *as if you had already achieved it* allows the unconscious mind to support you towards actual achievement of the outcome by filtering your senses to 'tune into' things that will help you to progress. There are so many pieces of information being picked up by your senses that your mind has to help you by filtering that information down to a far more manageable number. These are the points that you become aware of in a situation because our senses filter for what is most useful to us at that moment. For example, this may be through someone you might meet, by overhearing a conversation that someone has some useful information, or an opportunity that assists you in some way. This principle explains why two people can attend the same event, such as a meeting, and yet may perceive and recollect the details of the event quite differently.

Most people find it easiest to capture the detail of the first three aspects – visual, auditory and kinaesthetic, but if you are able to include olfactory and gustatory elements, this is useful to cover all five senses and firmly anchor the outcome you seek in your mind. Using your five senses to 'fill up your mind' is called Neuro-Linguistic Programming (NLP). NLP in essence means that what you say to yourself affects how you perceive the world.

To write such a detailed description, you have to be clear about what it is that you want and Template 8.4 provides structure to visualising your goal. Many people are quick to articulate what they do not want, however they can find it less easy to explain exactly what they do want. If you imagine that your unconscious mind, which filters your five senses, was a service provider, it would struggle to understand how to give you something you did not want. It would surely be far easier to help you by giving you something towards what you do want. The other reason for recommending complete clarity for your visualisation is because a person does not move forward while they remain 'double-minded', that is, stuck between two or more options. Your service provider still doesn't know what you really want so it is just easier to keep things as they are and hence nothing changes and we remain within this unfavourable scenario – effectively stuck.

Template 8.4 will help to visualise your goal and capture your description in great detail. After you have completed Template 8.4, read it over to yourself, both silently and aloud. Talk to your coaching partner about it as if you had already achieved it. By filling your mind with success on this particular matter, it will make it easier for your unconscious mind to filter your senses in the most appropriate way for you to notice how to move towards achieving this goal. Many coachees have tried this technique and been amazed at the success they have had!

Template 8.4 Goal visualisation

Visual Describe where you are; include location, colours, light, etc. What can you see happening? Who is there with you? How do they look?
Auditory What can you hear where you are? What are people saying to you about this? How do they sound?
Kinaesthetic How do you feel about this now you have achieved it? What do you now know and understand?
Olfactory What scent is there where you are? E.g. the smell of a candle, an animal, the countryside.
Gustatory What can you taste where you are? E.g. coffee, a certain type of food.

Conclusion

Social workers and student social workers can benefit from understanding and using coaching as an analytical skill to help solve problems encountered in their work. A coaching approach is also a valuable skill to use with service users and their families. Social workers will encounter individuals who are in some way stuck or unsure, or who may be inadvertently catastrophising their situation.

As part of their professional practice, social workers need to reflect upon their work to identify the learning from new perspectives and solve new problems for themselves and those they work with. Coaching and self-coaching are skills which can be used at all levels of a social work career, including in the management and supervision of other social workers.

9
Learning About and Learning From Service Users

Clare Stone and David R. Catherall

Introduction

Although the term 'service user' can be contentious, it has become common parlance within social work (Beresford, 2012:27). Service users are 'people who receive or are eligible to receive health, social care and welfare services ... either on a voluntary or compulsory basis' (Fleming, 2012:54). This can include those who approach a social care agency for advice and guidance, where the contact may not extend beyond one short telephone call, through to those who have engagement with a variety of services over many years. Informal carers and foster carers may be considered as a separate category from service users but within this chapter the term 'service user' is used as a generic term to cover both the users of services and their carers. This is because the social worker uses many of the same principles of assessment, support and engagement regardless of whether the individual is a service user in the traditional sense, or a carer of that person or even an extended family member. In a fostering team, for example, the practitioners may work with the looked-after child but the users of the service by and large are the foster carers, who are supported in their role as carers through training programmes and supervision. Regardless of the individual's role and 'status' they must all receive a professional service and therefore to consider them all as users of the service can be helpful and constructive.

In addition to being recipients of services, today in the UK service users, as is the case in other countries, are stakeholders in the management and evaluation of public services. Barnes and Cotterell (2012) claim that 'service user involvement in health and social care can be traced back to at least the early 1970s' and 'what was radical in the 1980s is now a well-established part of the health and social care system' (Barnes & Cotterell, 2012:XV & XXV). 'Service user involvement has been the subject of a huge amount of legislation and policy interest' and today service users are widely involved in the design and review of care services (Stone, Malihi-Shoja, McKeown & COMENSUS, 2013:227). User involvement has 'been part of the political, policy and professional scene for more than a generation in western societies' to the point where it is 'embodied in political and policy rhetoric, with requirements for them built into legislation, guidance and good practice manuals' (Beresford, 2012:20). A current example is The Care Act 2014 which sets out the responsibility of the Local Authority to begin 'with the assumption that the individual is best-placed to judge [their own] well-being' and therefore they must have regard for 'the individual's views, wishes, feelings and beliefs' (Care Act, 2014). This is because service users are experts through their own experience and as such are able to advise practitioners about their needs and how best to deliver a personalised service. This is the principle of the personalisation agenda which emphasises the service user's position within decision-making (Barnes & Cotterell, 2012). This bottom-up approach of user involvement 'moves beyond traditional top-down paternalistic approaches associated with the welfare state, to more user-centred provision' (Beresford, 2012:23). This starts from the assumption that we as social workers do not take the stance that we necessarily know best but, where appropriate, situate the power of knowledge with the service user and where at all possible, work in partnership with them.

Service user participation in care planning and service design is most important but that is not the primary focus of this chapter. This chapter takes the principles of user involvement and participation to focus on practitioner learning: learning about the commonality of the client group, the communities in which they live, or their solitary existence, and learning how to become a better social worker. To learn about and from service users we need to listen to their voice and attempt to really understand their views and experiences. Do you understand what it is really like to live on the fourth floor when you have arthritis? How do older adults purchase their weekly shopping when they live in a remote rural area? Do you know what life is like as the carer of a teenager with multiple disabilities? How does it feel when you have harmed your own children and for them to become subjects of child protection plans or forcibly removed from you? How does the individual feel about approaching your service for the first time? Does the service user feel they have a say in the planning of their care?

It is our experience that, due to the demands on practitioners' time, individuals will attempt to empathise with service users' situations but rarely is time devoted to meaningful engagement with service users to consider whether they really understand perspectives, their lives and their experience of being recipients of services. Practitioners can learn a great deal about and from service users but they need to take time to do this and carefully consider the method they employ. This chapter offers some practical activities to stimulate thinking about how social workers can learn from service users by acknowledging the service user as an expert through their own experience. Learning alongside service users is of course essential for those who are new to social work, however we also encourage the more experienced practitioners to reconsider the ideological and methodological approach promoted in this chapter. We offer the following activities with a note of caution as they cannot be used without careful thought about the impact upon both the practitioner and, of course, the service user.

Key Points

Social workers need to understand the service users and carers whom they work alongside and recognising their needs and understanding their perspectives is important in being able to provide a safe and effective service. By engaging in a meaningful way with the users of services social workers can develop their knowledge, skills and values.

- Practitioners can learn a great deal about and from service users.
- Practitioners need to dedicate time to learn and be motivated to learn.
- It is important to think about the learning methodology to ensure that the experience is appropriate for the service user and also the practitioner.

Significance for Social Work Practice

Working alongside service users does not always result in you understanding them, knowing what is in their best interests or being able to appropriately advocate on their behalf. This chapter is designed to encourage practitioners to consider how they can be creative in hearing the service user's authentic voice so they can learn about them and learn from them.

When you commence work in a new team or a different geographical area it is important to know who the users of the service are. There is no 'typical' service user as they are not a homogenous group but it may be possible to form an impression of the range of individuals who use the service, where they geographically live, the type of accommodation/environment they inhabit, the age range and other factors that make up the complex composition. Understanding these factors may ultimately enable you to provide a more accessible and needs-led service.

Services users must have a voice in all stages of the social work process and intervention. It is important to hear their voice within the assessment to help design and implement the most appropriate care and support services to meet their needs. They are experts about themselves and this ought to be recognised within the professional exchange and relationship. Service users are best placed to review and evaluate the service they receive and this includes the service they receive from the social worker. Actively seeking feedback and using that data has the potential to improve services, shape policy and help with the practitioner's professional development. The templates below provide suggestions to help you obtain rich and meaningful feedback from service users.

Whether the learner is a student, a new career social worker or a more experienced practitioner it is important to obtain a range of different perspectives and service users bring their unique and authentic voice to the learning process. Insights and feedback from those who receive services has significant value for professional development and may also be used for the purpose of practitioner assessment. Rather than guessing or interpreting views, service users can express their own perspectives, using their own language and intonations to make an authentic contribution to learning.

There is a range of creative ways of engaging service users (some of which are detailed below) and thought can be given to producing sustainable materials such as audio recorders or written narratives which can be used multiple times. Through engaging service users in teaching and within professional developmental activities, the social work values of respect, valuing individuals and working to rebalance power are all enacted. This may also result in the service user getting something positive out of the experience, such as an increased confidence and self-worth in the knowledge that they have made a valuable contribution to learning. When asked, service users said 'the best way to get really good social workers is if service users take part in their training'(Branfield, 2009:9). It is our experience that service users see the value of contributing to learning as it benefits the learner and ultimately impacts on the quality of service future service users will receive.

Although hearing the voice of service users is important and involving them in learning is advantageous there are important considerations to ensure that the experience is not tokenistic and that the individual is not disadvantaged in any way. If the purpose of the activity is solely for practitioner learning the service user must be informed of this and have the opportunity to withdraw at any point with the full knowledge that it will not have any impact on the services they receive now or in future. Consideration needs to be given to the cost to the service user in terms of time, travel and whether they will be paid or reimbursed. Some service users may require support to be involved and training may be appropriate.

Some organisations develop a trained and supported group of service users who are then empowered to sit on boards, act as consultants and even sit on interview panels. Although this is commendable practice it is important to work out whose voice it is that you need to hear and for what purpose. The trained person may be a suitable representative in some cases but they may have lost some authenticity and certainly will not be in a position to represent all service users in all cases. Avoid attending only to those who Beresford calls the 'vocal minority' because these tend to be the same individuals whose voice is the loudest (Beresford, 2013:5). You need to work out whose voice and whose feedback is most relevant to your learning and this may be those individuals who experience difficulty in communicating, those who are disengaged and even those who are angry, in crisis, unwell or irritated by your involvement.

Using in Practice

Social workers are employed in many different agency types and work with different service user groups and therefore it is important to consider the most appropriate way to engage with them. Some of the learning examples included within this chapter will require minimal amendment while others may be considered inappropriate. Therefore the practitioner–learner in partnership with their educator, assessor, line manager or supervisor needs to first decide what the learning goal is and how best to meaningfully involve service users in the process. These considerations must always be made in the context of the service user risk assessment, the sensitive nature of social work practice and agency policy, including health and safety guidance.

We have experienced some very creative ways in obtaining feedback from service users, eliciting rich and insightful data upon which the learner can reflect. We have also heard about learners who rip a page from an exercise book and ask the service users to 'write something about me'. This type of poor practice is oppressive to service users and does not result in feedback that can be relied upon. We have also had the pleasure of working alongside practitioners who embrace service user participation in all aspects of learning and professional development and some of the templates and exercises have been inspired by their work. Unfortunately there are some social workers who experience difficulty in thinking about sharing power with service users and fail to see the potential rewards for professional learning that working in partnership can provide. Even in child protection teams where the intervention may be mandated in legislation and the social worker may face hostility and disengagement, there are opportunities for learning from both the immediate and the extended members of the family.

Lancaster (2006) promotes the RAMPS framework comprising five principles to empower children to participate, have their say and be listened to:

- **R**ecognising children's many languages;
- **A**llocating communication spaces;
- **M**aking time;
- **P**roviding choice;
- **S**ubscribing to a reflective practice. (Lancaster, 2006:1)

It is our suggestion that these principles can be used to enable the voice of all service user groups to be heard. Think about the way the service user communicates, the environment of the intervention, afford the appropriate time and give individuals choice. Encourage them to draw upon their experiences and let them know that you value their contribution.

> **Case Study 9.1**
>
> The University of Central Lancashire (UCLan) in the North West of England has a very well established community engagement and service user support section called COMENSUS. In addition to working with initial training students on health and social care programmes they also have an educative role with experienced practitioners and postgraduate learners. They are stakeholders in programmes taking active participation in recruitment, admissions, teaching and assessment, and in the strategic management of programmes.
>
> There are multiple examples to draw upon where COMENSUS members have written vignettes and case studies, and spoken to learners about their experiences of being recipients of services. However we include here a learning scenario to inspire you to think about replicating some of the principles of meaningful service user involvement in education for social workers and social work practice.
>
> Instead of role play where one learner plays the role of a service user with whom their peer can practise and develop essential skills, COMENSUS arranges for those with real life experiences to take on the role of 'actor'. The service user draws upon their lived experience (both good and bad) to deliver real responses and understanding to the learning dyad. They may need to transfer and translate their experiences as relevant to the given scenario but it provides a more realistic learning experience to enable the social work learner to practise specific skills in a safe environment. The service user provides feedback on the skills employed, paying particular attention to communication and professionalism. The safety and support for the service user is considered and they are empowered to participate through the support of COMENSUS and the academic staff within the university.

> **Case Study 9.2**
>
> Kajal is a newly qualified social worker who settled into the team quickly and appears to be popular with peers, managers, other professionals and service users. She demonstrates high levels of emotional competence and always

appears to know what to say and how to respond but her desire to be liked results in her feeling less confident in situations where there is potential for conflict. In supervision she expresses to Brian (her manager) that she does not like to disappoint people and always strives to ensure that service users are 'happy' even when the outcome may not be as they had desired. Brian has observed Kajal in practice and is satisfied that she appropriately uses authority and she understands and enacts the balance between being a 'friendly professional' and a 'professional friend'. He has no concerns about her ability to maintain professional boundaries but suggests that they consider exploring her anxieties further by seeking meaningful feedback from service users. They used a range of strategies that included Kajal making notes by reflecting on her interactions with service users, paying particular attention to non-verbal cues. The questions on the service user feedback template below were used by Brian when he spoke to a service user after a joint visit and when speaking to others over the telephone, and the template was emailed to family members/carers.

Together Brian and Kajal analysed both the feedback and her notes to reflect upon what service users appeared to value about Kajal's practice. A service user wrote 'how can she know what it is like to be me??? she is young and has no children'. However in the context of the rest of the feedback from that individual and from other service users, Kajal was able to understand that she offered the best service possible and the service user's perspectives of her as an individual may on occasions be critical but that may not necessarily be a reflection of poor practice.

Service users appreciated her ability to explain process, turn up on time for appointments, keep them informed of what was going on and valued that she was open to hearing their opinions/views/concerns. Even those who were non-voluntary users of social work interventions and those who did not receive the outcomes they had desired, commented upon what we call the 'use of self'. Through hearing the authentic voice of those Kajal had been working with she began to feel less anxious about the need to be liked as she had a better understanding of what a professional relationship means in practice and the confidence in her ability to deliver a professional service.

Tools

Before using any of the tools below remember to think creatively, amend the examples and templates as required, balance the need to learn alongside the needs of the service users and ensure you are conforming to agency procedures.

Induction to a Building or Service

If you work within, or are a frequent visitor to, a residential establishment or day care service, a service user may be the most appropriate person to do the guided tour of the building. Pay attention to the language used and the explanations they offer about the use of rooms and the regime, as this may offer insight into how the service is perceived and experienced by the service users, which of course may differ considerably to employee perspectives. Template 9.1 provides questions to focus attention on thinking about how service users may experience and perceive the agency they deal with or the service they receive. These questions can also be adapted and where appropriate learners may have the opportunity to ask service users about their experiences. For example, a service user can be asked 'what do you value most about this service?'

Template 9.1 Induction to a building or service

What words or phrases are used by the users of the service?	
How do the service users appear to perceive and experience the service?	
What do they appear to value/benefit from/appreciate about the service?	
What aspects of the service do they appear to present in a less favourable light/wish to change?	
Additional thoughts and notes	

A Day in the Life of…

The saying 'don't judge me till you walk a mile in my shoes or live a day in my life' refocuses our attention onto the lived experience of others. Although it is not possible or advisable for practitioners to consider doing this for all of their service users, taking time to consider the lived experience/their daily life may offer new depths of understanding for practitioners. Service users could audio record or write a narrative about 'a day in the life of me' or the practitioner may spend some time with that individual in their usual environment doing usual activities. It would be helpful to focus on an aspect of their life that has relevance to your service and Template 9.2 offers a framework for reflecting on this. Earlier in the chapter we asked how older adults purchase their weekly shop when they live in a remote rural area. Try the journey yourself to the local shop (using the same mode as the service user for example walking or using the bus), consider the physical demands and whether the shop actually sells adequate provisions. Consider the growing use of internet shopping in rural areas and how this might affect an elderly person and also those new to computer use.

You may also want to consider the reality of life for service users at particularly difficult times of the day. The morning or bedtime routines of children are often significant stressors for parents. Through observation of this, in the home setting, a social worker can begin to understand the demands and challenges faced by a family, and can ensure that these are considered fully in the assessment and the planning for service provision. Template 9.2 encourages learners to think about a day in the life of a service user or carer and extends beyond the physical, emotional and mental health to take into account the lived experience, the environment and the community. The aim is to gain a deeper understanding of life as lived by another individual.

Template 9.2 A day in the life of a service user or carer

What times of day are particularly challenging for the individual?	
What practical/domestic tasks are particularly challenging for the individual?	
Is there anything to note about their immediate living environment/facilities?	
Is there anything to note about the community in which they live (transport, isolation, services, support)?	
What else is of significance in relation to this service user's lived experience/daily life?	
What would make a difference to them?	
What services and support may be appropriate in relation to my role as a social worker?	
Additional thoughts and notes	

The Community We Live In

A similar exercise to the journey to the shop is where the service user orientates you to their community. The individual gives you a guided tour and points out key services such as the post office, health centre, and other services relevant to your work. Like the exercise of induction to a building, pay attention to the language used, their explanations and experiences. Not only do you begin to learn where things are but you can also experience how easy or difficult it is to access services. It is easy to be critical of a parent who arrives late for the contact sessions with their child until you have insight into the challenges of the journey on foot or via two buses. The questions in Template 9.3 encourage deeper reflection on how service users perceive and experience their community and how this impacts on well-being.

Template 9.3 The community we live in

What words or phrases are used by the users of the service to describe the community?	
How do the service users appear to perceive and experience their community?	
What do they appear to value about the community in which they live?	
What aspects of the community do they appear to present in a less favourable light/wish to change?	
What aspects of their community appear to challenge their daily life, potential for change/growth/independence?	
What services and support may be appropriate in relation to my role as a social worker?	
Additional thoughts and notes	

An exercise that works well with students is to provide them with a map onto which they draw the location of all the places that have been listed for them to find. The map exercise enables the learner to locate key services and resources, and become familiar with the environment. During the induction of students, a learning disability service provides them with a street map and asks them to find the number of the supported tenancy house on a particular street. Those who have limited experience of working within learning disabilities soon learn a valuable lesson when they cannot find a house that meets their expectations, as many set out to find a 'care home' or large institution with a sign outside.

Another way to involve service users in educating social workers about their community and life is to ask them to do a photo montage or do some video filming. A young person can use a disposable camera or their smart phone to capture all of the things they like and value, and those things they wish to change. A collage of pictures from a magazine may also capture similar insight into a person's life, environment, goals and dreams. Imagine the powerful image created by a service user who is given the brief to pictorially represent 'the community I live in'. Negotiate with the service user how they will share images with you, what they will be used for, how the images will be stored and who will see them.

It may be appropriate to be present while the service user photographs or videos as they have the opportunity to explain to you why they have chosen to capture certain images. You can ask them questions such as 'why is that important to you?'

Who are the Users of our Service?

Not all service users are the same and they do not all come with the same history or circumstances. It is important for practitioners to think about the range of people who access their services but it may also be helpful to consider similarities and common features. Take time to consider how people came to need your service and what other services they have passed through and have contact with. One technique is to draw a time line marking significant points along their trajectory.

There are other obvious learning techniques for understanding who the service users are, such as interviewing to construct a case history or pen picture. Life story work is often used with children and the same principles can be used with adults. The practitioner can work with a service user or family to construct a life narrative, which provides insight into their history, successes, career, family, aspirations and challenges. The depth of understanding gained by reconstructing one's life can help with best interest decisions and can guide both immediate care provision and future care planning. Another way to develop insight into who the users of your service are is to read literature written by and about service users and this is further explored in Chapter 11, entitled 'Book Groups and Fiction: A "Novel" Approach to Teaching and Learning'.

Feedback

It is common practice for social care and social work services to issue compliments, complaints and comments questionnaires and the data generated can be most insightful to influence service development. It is very important to understand how those in receipt of services experience the quality, quantity and general standards of care. However, it is also necessary to capture service users' experiences of the people involved in their care. As a developing social worker, it is essential to take time to capture feedback about how service users experience your intervention, then analyse that feedback and respond to it.

> Obtaining feedback from the people who are supported by social work services is essential to support critical reflection and to aid practitioners in improving their practice. Seeking feedback both formally and informally is the basis of the relationship building and effective partnership working that become the toolkit of intuitive working. (Department for Education and Skills for Care, no date)

To obtain rich and meaningful feedback it is important to consider how service users are approached and what they are asked to do. There may be situations where it is appropriate to leave a questionnaire with a service user and ask them to return it to you in a prepaid envelope but in other situations alternative approaches would be more advantageous. The following templates and tips are to be used as guides and it is important that you amend them to make the approach, format and recording appropriate to the service user you approach.

Feedback considerations:

- Will the service user understand what you are asking? Take time to structure questions and guidance and use a medium and language that is appropriate. If you are asking questions, make them open-ended not closed and avoid leading questions. Do not use jargon, acronyms or technical terms.

- Make it clear what the feedback is for. State that it is for your professional development.

- Explain who will see the feedback. Make it clear to the service user at the outset if you are going to share the feedback with anyone or if it is to be used for the purpose of a testimonial or assessment.
- Ensure the service user knows they do not have to provide feedback. They need to understand that the feedback they provide (or decline to provide) will have no adverse influence on current or future services.
- Does the service user need someone to help them provide the feedback?
- Consider how the service user may feel about giving feedback and whether there is any undue influence or pressure. Plan whether you are going to be present when they generate the feedback and consider if it is more appropriate for someone else to approach the service user to obtain the feedback. If you work in a setting where there are a few service users you may wish to ask for collective feedback or arrange for one service user to obtain feedback from a second.
- Think about how service users can provide anonymous feedback if they wish. However, if a service user knows the feedback is going to be shared with a second person and they choose to insert their name it would be very disrespectful to anonymise the data. Only blank out identifying features if you have concerns about confidentiality/data protection.
- Complimentary feedback is nice, however rich feedback is more helpful for professional development so invite critical comments and suggestions for improvement.
- Don't just ask those you think you have the best relationships with or those who are easiest to approach. It is important to get a range of views and you may be surprised by the insightful feedback generated.
- Think about the length of time it will take the service users to provide feedback, are there any resource implications, will they enjoy providing feedback and are they likely to consider it worthy of their time. Do not unduly inconvenience the service users and explain why the feedback will be of help to you.
- Remember feedback can take many forms and does not have to be a completed paper questionnaire. Think about interviews, use of

technology, picture cards and drawings. Sometimes the best feedback is spontaneous and non-verbal. The fact that a young person turns up on time for the appointment may say more about their perception of you than could ever be captured in words on a form. It is therefore essential for you to be aware of reading non-verbal cues.

All of the templates within this chapter can be adapted in terms of content and how they are used. They can be used as questionnaires (on paper or electronically) or the questions can be used in discussion or as an interview, face-to-face or over the telephone. Children may enjoy holding up smiley and sad-faced cards; drawing on large sheets of paper and using post-it notes can make the activities more fun. Remember it is by asking the right question in an appropriate way that elicits rich, full and useful feedback.

You can draw images such as these onto feedback forms or onto cards which can be held up or pointed to.

Template 9.4 is a standard service user or carer feedback sheet which has been designed to focus on the professionalism of the social worker/student rather than the services being received. It informs the service users and carers about the purpose of the feedback and there is a space to clearly inform who may see the feedback and how it will be used. For example a student may state that the completed form will be included within their portfolio for the purpose of the assessment of their placement.

Template 9.4 Standard service user or carer feedback template

The purpose of this sheet is to guide the social worker on their development and to help improve practice. Your responses are anonymous and will be kept confidential. Your comments will be most useful to the social worker's learning.
The social worker will be asked to consider your feedback and may include this form in ....
If you need help with this form, please ask.

(Continued)

Template 9.4 (*Continued*)

All questions are optional	
Did the social worker introduce themselves and make it clear why you were meeting with them?	YES NO Any comments
Do you feel that the social worker planned for the visit and had a clear understanding of the background to the visit?	YES NO Any comments
Did the social worker put you at your ease?	YES NO Any comments
Was the social worker aware of your support needs? (These may be disabilities, cultural needs, religious, gender, sexuality, etc.)	YES NO Any comments
Did the social worker listen and understand what you said?	YES No Any comments
Did the social worker treat you with respect?	YES NO Any comments
Comment on the quality of advice and/or information given by the social worker	GOOD AVERAGE POOR Any comments

LEARNING ABOUT AND LEARNING FROM SERVICE USERS 151

Did you understand at the end of the meeting if any action was going to be taken?	YES NO Any comments
Did you feel the visit was worthwhile?	YES NO Please comment and explain
Is there any other information you wish to give the social worker to guide them in their learning and development?	Please comment
Thank you for taking the time to complete this feedback sheet	

Template 9.5 is a shortened and edited version of the template devised by COMENSUS (a service user-led hub at the University of Central Lancashire) to illustrate how pictures and smiley faces can be used.

Template 9.5 Easy read feedback template

This sheet is to guide the social worker and help them to be good at their job. What you say will only be used to help them and you don't have to give your name.

What you say is important to us, as it will help the social worker to learn. The social worker will keep this form safe.

If you need help with this form, please ask. Thank you for filling in this form.

<u>All questions are optional</u>

The social worker can insert a picture of themselves here to remind the service user who the feedback is about	
Did you know why you were meeting with the social worker?	😊 ☹ 😐

(Continued)

Template 9.5 (*Continued*)

How did you feel with the social worker?	Safe ✗ ✓ Comfortable ✗ ✓ Trusted the social worker ✗ ✓ Felt understood ✗ ✓
Did the social worker listen to what you said?	😊 ☹ 😐 Any comments?
Did the social worker spend time with you?	😊 ☹ 😐 Any comments?
Did the social worker give you good advice?	😊 ☹ 😐 Any comments?
Would you like to tell the social worker anything else?	Please comment

Conclusion

Regardless of the method employed to understand who the service users are, their histories, where they live and the challenges they face on a day-to-day basis, the important thing is to move beyond hearing their story. Do not collect their views without considering what learning can be extracted from the generated data. Obtaining their perspectives and collecting feedback is a means to an end and not an end in itself. You need to engage in reflective practice and ask yourself a series of questions. You may first wish to consider the service user's involvement:

- How do you think the person being supported felt about giving this feedback?
- What difference do you think being involved in providing feedback made to the person? (DFE & SFC, no date)

Then you need to focus upon the content of feedback:

- Does the service offered meet their needs and expectations?
- What lessons can I learn from this feedback in general?
- What insight does this feedback give me in relation to this particular individual/family?
- What does that mean in relation to other service users?
- How will this knowledge impact on my professional practice?
- What learning and development needs have I identified as a result of this?
- What is my learning plan as a result of the feedback (how and when am I going to address those points identified above)?

A repeated message in this book is that transformative learning requires more than merely having an experience, and therefore practitioners must decide what needs to be learnt and how it needs to be learnt, and reflect on the experience and amend practice as a result of new insights. Learning about service users and learning from service users has the potential to improve service delivery and inform the development of the professional self.

10
Developing Digital Competence for Practice

Joanne Westwood and Amanda M. L. Taylor

@jlwestwood
@AMLTaylor66

Introduction

Social work practitioners engage in practice that is complex and uncertain. They work with all manner of problems as they arise and they meet these challenges head-on with determination and creativity. They are frequently introduced to information and circumstances that take them out of their comfort zones and adjust and adapt as necessary to issues that require new ways of thinking and working in conditions that are shaped by what is changing within the practice landscape. Digitalisation is one such change. The digital era is characterised by the increasing use of technologies, which are becoming more and more integral to the lived experience. This requires a practical and ethical response from the social work profession that is both competent and confident in nature. We pause at this point to offer definitions and outline our understanding of key terms.

Social Media

Boyd and Ellison (2007) define social media as: 'web-based services that allow individuals to construct a public or semi-public profile within a bounded system, articulate a list of other users with whom they share a connection, view and traverse their list of connections and those made by others within the system' (p. 209).

Social media is designed to facilitate user interaction between users to create and communicate news, information and ideas and necessarily involves online social and professional networking between individuals. Developments in web technologies during the last decade have made it possible for social media users to connect and interact with web content and with each other (Fang et al., 2014). Social media is distinguished from other online activity in terms of the ability of users to create and contribute online materials (Kimball & Kim, 2013). The trend towards increased use of social media is upwards among young people (Lafferty, 2015) as is ownership of smart devices which is increasing and overtaking ownership of other hardware, for example, personal computers or laptops (GWI, 2014).

Social Networking Sites

Social Networking Sites: (SNSs) are online spaces designed and used to host individual or organisational profiles, these might include written content, photographs, video and audio materials. There are some very popular SNSs, such as Facebook (www.facebook.com), which has upwards of 1.4 billion accounts (Statista, 2015). Facebook users can invite other users to view their profile, connect and engage in dialogue and discussions using Instant Messaging, (IM). Facebook users can establish online groups and a range of other communication strategies and tools, which allow them to upload and share visual and audio materials. A blog is another example of an SNS and enables users to publish views and opinions, thoughts and reflections. Blogs such as Tumblr (https://www.tumblr.com/) with more than 230 million active blogs (Statista 2015) can be shared or restricted so that they are only accessible by certain individuals. Micro-blogging also places restrictions on the number of characters that can be used in posts. Twitter (www.twitter.com/) is the largest micro blog site with 288 monthly accounts (Statista 2015) and has a limit of 140 characters. In terms of the distribution and use of SNSs across the globe, there are clear differences between ownership and use in developing and developed countries, and a digital divide within developed countries (Whatis.com? 2015).

Digital Competence and Digital Literacy

As digital technology develops we need to acquire skills and knowledge to navigate, select and interact with it comfortably and with confidence. JISC (2015) define digital literacy in terms of the capability a person has for embracing digital tools in all areas of their lives. JISC suggest that there are several elements of digital literacy, which include learning skills, ITC literacy, career and identity management, information literacy, digital scholarship (academic or professional), media literacy and communication and collaboration (i.e. participation in digital networks). White and Le Cornu (2011) distinguish between those who are confident and familiar with using digital technology (digital residents) and those who are starting to engage with technology (digital visitors).

Web2.0

DiNucci (1999) defines Web 2.0 in terms of user interactivity with the content, which is universally accessible through a standard interface. The World Wide Web was initially made up of largely static websites that hosted information equivalent to printed material. Web 2.0 has much more sophisticated capabilities which are based on user engagement and interaction with the technology as well as the creation of content.

Virtual Learning Environment

A Virtual Learning Environment (VLE) is an online space designed to host learning and development materials and for some elements of interaction between learners and educators. Examples of VLEs used in universities include Moodle and Blackboard.

Key Points

Digital technologies are increasingly used within social work education, and within social work practice, and it is therefore essential for social workers to consider:

> - the range of technologies available and the appropriate use of these within social work;

- their online presence and activity as private individuals and as professionals;
- what is meant by digital competence for social work practice;
- ethics and issues of conduct for social work practice; and
- their engagement with and reflections on using social media in their practice.

Significance for Social Work Practice

There is a growing local and global network within the social work profession that is made up of service-users, students, practitioners, managers and academics who connect and engage using social networking sites (SNS) such as Twitter, Facebook and LinkedIn. At no other time in the history of the profession has social work education and practice been connected to this extent; nor has there been a medium to collapse the restraints previously imposed by geographic boundaries. It is as a result of these connections that relationships have been built, practices have been changed and innovations have been developed. Indeed, the Chief Social Work for England (Adults) acknowledges (through the medium of Twitter) such developments:

> Social media's greatest achievement has been its connectivity, the ability to share and respond to conversations, ideas and observations instantly and, in so doing, foster online communities of like-minded people. Twitter in particular has demonstrated this capacity to engage and educate – in surprising and unexpected ways. (Romeo, 2015)

Baker et al. (2014) advises that 'Social work must overcome its historical reluctance to embrace ICT if it is to remain relevant in the era of the network society' (Baker et al., 2014: 468). With that in mind this chapter provides the opportunity for students, practitioners, managers and practice educators alike to reflect upon their digital presence and provide recent examples of social media and technologies as they are being utilised in social work education and practice. We take a systemic approach, considering practitioner, agency and digital technology to our thinking and as a result start by asking you to pause and reflect on the following questions:

- Which social media and technologies do you use?

- What is the purpose of your engagement with each?
- What is your ongoing professional development and practice approach in a digital sense?

It is within these reflections that you will begin to consider how you position yourself in relation to new digital technologies and social media in terms of your practice and your ongoing professional development. Social work education is increasingly being required to respond to technological changes that are pertinent to practice and qualifying students will have had some level of exposure and interaction with a wide range of digital technologies as they enter the workforce. However, in many ways engagement with these mediums is still in its infancy and we are all navigating our way through the changes as they occur. Given the speed and magnitude of these changes it is important to have an understanding of how digital technologies are shaping the practice landscape and a grasp of what this means for you as a practitioner and your practice approach.

Digital capabilities and specifically social media offer practitioners the opportunities to connect and interact with an easily accessible knowledge network as never before. People who use social services are also embracing these affordances, which improve their ability to access information, online and peer support, and advice. The developments in communication offer opportunities for practitioners to engage with service users in different ways using digital technologies, but this brings a host of issues to the fore, which must be considered for social work practice to stay true to its ethical values base. At no other time has this been more relevant given recent cases publicised in the media where an increasing number of social work professionals are being called before their regulatory body to account for their online activities and behaviours. The education and professional development trajectory in social work is defined and regulated by professional bodies from across all four nations of the UK. Within each grouping there are slight variations in the nature of the language and the approaches taken that describe, shape and govern social work practice. These variations can be seen clearly within policy, which, by and large, is demographically and politically determined. Despite these variations there are universal skills which are core to effective practice, and fundamental abilities that enable practitioners to respond ethically and appropriately to need and risk in a social work context.

Regulatory bodies, such as the Health Care Professionals Council, Scottish Social Service Council, Care Council for Wales and the Northern Ireland Social Care Council, together with, for example, the British Association of Social Work (BASW), are affected by issues arising from digital technology and its application in practice. BASW (2012) published its own social media policy in order to clarify its position and provide clear advice and information for the profession. Despite the fact there may be differences in how each of the nations address technology-associated issues and practice, it is important that any policy and practice developments are underpinned by codes of conduct, bolstered by the professional value base.

Regulatory bodies in the UK and beyond make specific reference to social media usage and require registrants to adhere to their standards and codes of conduct. Social work educators and students need to consider how they engage with social media and make choices about how they use it, based on a set of shared values, including trust, respect and confidentiality, all of which are central to social work practice. There are barriers that deter engagement with technology and social media specifically, including lack of skills and knowledge about how it can be utilised in a professional environment. Online contact is also distinct from real time face-to-face contact. Fang et al. (2014) identify these differences as: persistence, as online content is permanent and immediately searchable; and replicable, in that it can be scaled up and made quickly available to other users. There are risks for misunderstanding communications that are posted online and thus the potential for conflict and disagreement. Practitioners need to be informed about the need for secure and private online spaces so that they do not breach the codes of conduct. Goldkind and Wolf, in their (2014) analysis, argue that developments in technology have changed the ways in which we communicate and engage with others, and the social work profession needs to review the way values are shaped and revised by technology.

It will be useful at this point to pause and think:

➤ About which policies and procedures inform your online behaviours in your workplace?

- About what is your understanding of 'professionalism' in digital online spaces?
- About the knowledge, skills and values that you draw on when you engage in digital and/or social media technologies?
- If there are any ethical tensions regarding online practices that you have experienced or anticipate?

Using in Practice

The complexity of the Internet, the vast range of technological tools and their relevance to social work education and practice is a pressing concern across the profession. It is therefore important that we each take responsibility for what we know, paying due attention to how this knowledge is being employed to ensure that practice is ethical and effective. Each of the above pause-and-think activities are designed to enable you to unpack your current levels of digital competence, as well as provide you with an opportunity to consider that which you might need to address in terms of technology-based professional development. The mapping tool below is a useful way to reflect upon competence and digital activity.

The following activity is based on the work of White and Le Cornu (2011) who have developed a 'mapping tool' aimed at assisting learners to characterise their online abilities, and reflect upon their digital activity. Engaging in this mapping exercise, in light of your earlier reflections, will further assist you to define and chart your technology usage, online intentions and behaviours. It should also serve as a prompt to explore the layers that make up the digitally confident and competent practitioner. Charted below (Figure 10.1) is an example of a social work practitioner's technologies usage. It outlines the personal and the professional context in which technologies are employed, highlighting, among many things, boundary issues that might exist at these early stages of reflective analysis. Again, pause and think here to consider where you might situate yourself in terms of your use of social media mapping using the matrix in Figure 10.1 which has been adapted from White and Le Cornu, (2011).

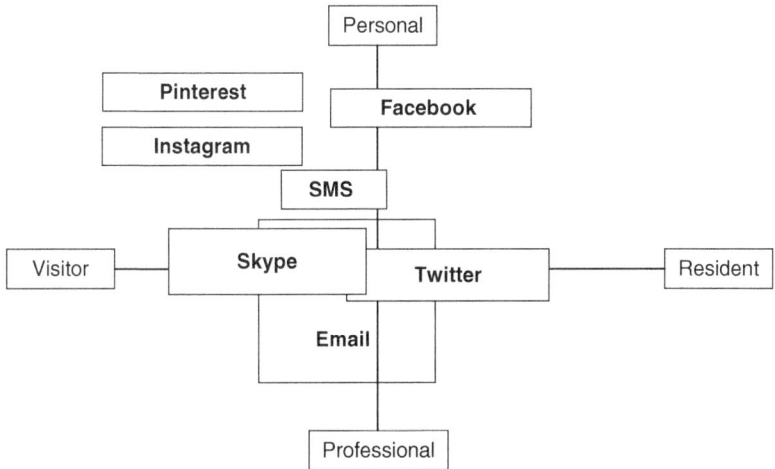

Figure 10.1 Mapping technology usage

As the matrix illustrates there is overlapping and crossing of boundaries between personal and professional online engagement and activity as well as distinctions between which social media platforms are used and in what context. Prensky (2001) was interested in the difference between learners who have grown up with technologies and those who have not. Prensky (2001) coined the terms 'digital natives' and 'digital immigrants' to describe these learners, suggesting that these positions were primarily fixed, with the former to some degree favouring technologies and the latter either tolerating or embracing them, in equal measure (p. 2). White and Le Cornu's (2011) work, to a larger extent, challenges these perceptions, resolving that digital literacies are not fixed. Indeed, they propose a fluid conceptualisation of the profile of an individual navigating the digital age, a concept that is not related to age or life stage. They discuss digital abilities in terms of 'literacies', and suggest the 'visitor' or 'resident' terminology as a more accurate and inclusive typology to describe technology users. Visitors are those who are tentatively enquiring or finding out about the digital landscape, whereas residents are comfortable and confident in their knowledge and immerse themselves willingly in the digital landscape (White & Le Cornu, 2011: np). Their work has recently developed beyond the original single (Visitor–Resident) axis and now includes a vertical axis (Figure 10.1) that links reflection to the context, (Personal–Professional) as well as the content of technology usage.

The scope of this accessible tool sits well within the social work education context as it affords the learner/practitioner an opportunity to fully consider the technologies they use. The tool allows the individual to identify any conflicts of interest, potential blurring of boundaries and to chart their professional development. These reflections should be set within the relevant professional standards for practice, alongside the social work value base. Agencies and organisations cannot expect their employees to develop competence and confidence in using digital technologies unless they are supportive of this advancement. Employers should provide an environment which enables this development, and promote organisational strategies and good governance, including service users in these developments as well as legal services and human resources departments (Kimball & Kim, 2013).

There are a number of areas of development that require due consideration, here we discuss digital competence and professionalism. Digital competence requires us to have a set of digital literacies. Belshaw (2014) argues that rather than literacies being acquired individually, skills are developed within a context, and there is a continuum from becoming digitally competent to digitally literate. According to Belshaw (2014) there are several elements of digital literacy and each may feature more strongly in one context than another. As the technology develops we need to find ways to navigate through these and sometimes this is simultaneous as we acquire and consolidate digital skills, knowledge and competence.

Sapey as far back as 1997 explained that

> unless social workers do become involved in the ways in which new technologies are used within organizations, they will fail to influence its impact upon their clients and may further fail to control the way in which computers affect the nature of social work itself in the future. (p. 803)

It is commonplace for practitioners in the field to use ITC to record case information (databases i.e. Liquid Logic), communicate with colleagues (email) and service users (telephone, mobile telephone and even texting). There are examples of practitioners using Apps to engage with children who are looked-after to enable them to contribute to their reviews and make complaints (Fursland, 2014). There is an increasing range of materials available for training and development using Apps which are easily accessed using smart technology; for example, a child development App which contains information on children's developmental milestones, theoretical frameworks, key legislation and policy relevant to work with children and families. This child development App is useful for learners while on practice placement and for practitioners because the content facilitates critical reflection and aids evidence-based decision-making (Learning Pool, 2014). Advances in technology and digital citizenship are also pushing forward the development of new ways of consulting with, and gaining feedback from, people who use social services. Research suggests that local authorities are engaging with digital technologies and social media in customer services-orientated aspects of their work (BDO, 2012, 2013) however they need support to try out ideas and implement new methods of working with people who use public services. In terms of social work practice, guidance on using digital tools and specifically social media should be co-produced in partnership with service users (Kimball & Kim, 2013).

It is important to pay attention to the digital divide, and issues of exclusion and inclusion. Aside from the differences in access because of coverage, there are clear divisions between those who have access to technology, which enables them to pay bills and order shopping online, and those who do not. While the trend towards smart phone ownership is upwards, there are still issues related to income and accessibility, that determine who can and who cannot access the Internet, for example, people who live in rural areas where there is limited or slow connection or no access to broadband. There may also be reluctance among people to engage with digital technologies, and economic barriers for some which prevent ownership and access.

Case Studies

The following two case studies illustrate that there are clear benefits for social workers, service users and carers, in engaging with and using social media. The important factor in these practice-based case studies is that considerable time and energy has gone into thinking through the development of these tools in terms of ethics, values and skills development. As a result clear boundaries and guidance for practice have been developed to support the technological elements of the work.

Case Study 10.1: **The Social Work Social Media App**

The Social Media for Social Work App (Singh Cooner, 2013) was designed to encourage discussion about values and ethical issues posed by social media in social work practice. The App examines several practice-related case studies and is accompanied by a supplementary teaching and learning guide and workbook for social work educators and practitioners. The App uses a games-based study approach to encourage discussion and debate. For example, in the first scenario practitioners argue that they are too busy to attend training on social media, and then the activity goes on to illustrate how service users seek advice about using social media and how social workers benefit from advice shared on social media. The App is designed to stimulate discussion about how practitioners need to be aware of how they are perceived. The questions posed by the App also require reflection about using social media in our private lives, for example, in another scenario a worker posts photographs of himself after a night out drinking and other team members discuss the appropriateness of this. The scenarios provide the impetus for team discussions about how they and service users use social media, and provide opportunities to explore the tensions and challenges which practitioners face in their work as well as supporting the development of practical skills in terms of navigating through the features and activities.

Case Study 10.2: **Facebook for Foster Carers in Aberdeenshire**

In Aberdeenshire, the foster and adoption teams established a Facebook group to promote fostering opportunities across the council as there was a shortage of foster carers. As well as acting as a recruitment tool, the Facebook group connects existing foster carers to each other. Foster care recruitment has increased year on year and the majority of initial enquiries about fostering now come through this social media channel. The analytical tools available for using this medium allow the council to plan their campaigning and recruitment strategies. The Facebook page now includes information about training for foster carers. All social media posts that are published on the Facebook account are approved by the Council's communication team. In Aberdeenshire's case a small dedicated team take responsibility via a rota system to maintain the page, post activities and respond to queries from potential carers.

Resources

We have compiled a range of digital and social media resources below. There are various blogs and online magazines, together with links to individuals, organisations and sites, which host easily accessible learning materials. There are also resources which will be useful for developing social media policies and strategies:

BASW (2012). Social Media Policy. http://cdn.basw.co.uk/upload/basw_34634-1.pdf

Community care magazine – a widely read online social work, social care publication and resource for practitioners, students, organisations and academics, based in the UK http://www.communitycare.co.uk/

Facebook : Setting up a Facebook account https://www.facebook.com/help/345121355559712/

Guardian social care: http://www.theguardian.com/social-care-network Twitter @Guardiansocialcare

Health Care Professions Council (2012). Focus on standards: Social Networking Sites http://www.hcpc-uk.org/Assets/documents/100035B7Social_media_guidance.pdf

JSWEC: UK Joint Social Work Education and Research. Twitter: @jswec

JusticeforLB Twitter: @JusticeforLB was established in February 2014 to campaign for Justice. http://justiceforlb.org/

Martin Webbers Blog 'Musings of a social work academic'. Martin is a Reader in Social Work at the University of York. 'This blog arises from my work and my reflections upon it. One of its aims is to help to bridge the gap between the academic and practice fields of social work', http://martinwebber.net/ Twitter : @mgoat73

NISCC (2015). NISCC Apps http://niscc.info/index.php/14-employers/236-mobile-apps-all-niscc-apps

Online Masters in Social Work Programmers Resource Page http://www.onlinemswprograms.com/top-social-work-professors-on-twitter.html

SSSC (2012). What is social media? http://workforcesolutions.sssc.uk.com/new/docs/What_is_Social_Media_-_transcript.pdf

Social Work/Social Care & Media (2015). Knowledge Community of Practice http://swscmedia.com/

Social Work Book Groups Storify Page https://storify.com/AMLTaylor66/the-use-of-book-clubs-in-social-work-education

Social Work Helper – 'a progressive digital publication providing news, information, and resources related to social issues, social good, and human rights', http://www.socialworkhelper.com/subscribe-weekly-helper/

SWAPBox – a space for 'storing, managing and publishing your social policy and social work teaching resources on the web. Share handouts, exercises, podcasts, videos and anything else you can imagine!' http://www.swapbox.ac.uk/

The Masked AMHP whose blog aims to 'share experience of being an Approved Mental Health Professional (AMHP) (what used to be called an Approved Social Worker, or ASW), practicing under the Mental Health Act 1983 (as recently amended)' http://the-maskedamhp.blogspot.co.uk/2009_03_01_archive.html

The National Elf Service – this 'website will help you find just what you need to keep up-to-date with all of the important and reliable mental health research and guidance', http://www.nationalelfservice.net/elf/mental/

The Social Care Elf, 'jointly funded by Minervation Ltd, the Personal Social Services Research Unit at the LSE and the NIHR School for Social Care Research as part of Social Care Evidence in Practice (SCEiP project). Supporting organisations include Making Research Count, the Social Services Research Group and the Social Care Institute for Excellence, http://www.thesocialcareelf.net/

Twitter: How to set up a Twitter account https://support.twitter.com/articles/100990-signing-up-with-twitter#

Whoseshoes https://whoseshoes.wordpress.com/ Twitter: @Whose Shoes

Conclusion

The influence of technology on social work practice is an issue being discussed at all levels, in terms of the professional standards for practice, demographic changes and the availability of resources. Technological advances also serve to influence how social work is delivered. In Scotland, for example, the Institute for research and Innovation in Social Services (IRISS) work with social work agencies to develop new methods of working which draw on technology. Call centres, online counselling services, and communication through digital, including audio and visual technologies, are likely to increase in the future and there are some key benefits in terms of speed and accessibility. There is also the potential that the social work role will be compromised as more generic digital literacy skills are required to deliver this. The social work profession and leaders therefore have a responsibility to ensure that they are engaged with innovations and developments for social work practice. It is crucial that social work leaders seek out opportunities to explore how they can capitalise on their services and resources in creative ways that embrace the benefits of technological advances. This needs to be done in such a way as to complement and enhance the relational aspects of interventions. Digital technological innovations cannot and should not replace the crucial human elements of social work practice.

11
Book Groups and Fiction: A 'Novel' Approach to Teaching and Learning

Amanda M. L. Taylor

Introduction

As Addison explains, 'reading is a basic tool in the living of a good life' (no date, cited in Sousa, 2011:137) and in social work we are finding that fiction can provide us with an immeasurable amount of material in relation to the human condition, and an insight into the lived experiences of others. Books can draw the reader into spaces and places where all nature of thoughts, feelings, emotions and challenges are felt. They can confirm, and also confront, our ideas, ideals, values and beliefs and force us to question the world and how we fit within it. They replicate almost every aspect of life possible, with some even impossible to imagine, or so one might think. They allow us to feel, at times when our feelings are inaccessible, they keep us safe when we might need to escape; there is little that cannot be found within their covers. Indeed as Petrosky (1986) states, it encourages, 'Critical thinking [and] makes meaning ... [through] correlating it to life experiences' (p.3). Contrast this with the vast amounts of information written by social work practitioners as they listen to, record and report on the lives of others. Lives that present in many forms, that take many paths; those that can prompt and arouse a great deal of the same types of responses as a fictive text. Hence the reason why fiction is being discussed here – it is a learning medium that can provide the reader with a safe context in which to explore the lived experiences of others, only in this instance from a less connected position.

The idea for book groups as a methodology in social work education evolved out of an experimental teaching activity within a module of learning; one that sought to cultivate effective reading habits as a means to accessing, digesting and consolidating knowledge. It is a method underpinned by the thinking and works of Mortiboys (2011) who cites the benefits of, 'use[ing]... stories' explaining them as teaching tools that are, 'pivotal... [to the] gaining, retaining or indeed regaining [of] attention' (p. 56). Walker (2008) furthers this proposition by prompting educators to assist students to, 'develop the habit of reading' and makes the point that this can be achieved through appraising 'novels or less academic books' (cited in Scourfield & Taylor 2013:1). In addition, and in keeping with these pedagogic findings, the aforementioned teaching experiment aimed to support those students for whom reading can be a challenge, who often cite this learning medium as a demanding, or laborious task. Furthermore, these difficulties are frequently contextualised in relation to the volume of required reading when engaged with professional level study. It is often assumed that reading is something that comes naturally to all students – something that they all do, and something that they are all motivated to do – when in fact there is diversity in the reading tendencies of learners within any learning population (Parrot & Cherry, 2011). Nonetheless, given the nature of academic study, and that of continued professional development, reading is an activity that can neither be escaped nor avoided; and when it is, there are negative impacts on academic success (Wernersbach et al., 2014).

Learning for practice in social work is a commitment necessary from the outset of the initial training right through the practitioners' career trajectory. It is a continuous journey of knowledge acquisition that relies heavily on accessibility through innovation, particularly for busy practitioners. Book groups and the reading of fiction, are accessible and contemporary learning methodologies that offer a means of addressing the needs of a range of learners, at various stages of the learning journey. Given the connection between reading and the development of knowledge, fostering reading and nurturing readers is significant to the augmenting of understandings and achievement more generally. Therefore, being required to read, commonly referred to as compulsory reading (Meyer et al., 2012), and having the opportunity to discuss the content with an educator and peers, can be both an engaging, and a dynamic learning experience. Through the modular teaching experiment mentioned, it was found that, as a result of encouraging students to read fiction and to view the fictional content as a case file, learners were able to read with purpose and to explore the content from a practice perspective, which resulted in a deeper level of learning, that was to a greater extent experiential in nature (Taylor, 2014b).

I have written at length about the use of book groups in social work education in a number of publications (Scourfield & Taylor, 2013; Taylor, 2014a; Taylor, 2014b; Taylor in Brewer & Hogarth, 2015) outlining their purpose, relevance and usefulness as a teaching and learning medium. However, in this book the motivation to write comes from the testimonies of students, practitioners, academics and researchers who have engaged with a national social work book group; whose feedback has shaped, influenced and evidenced that the reading of fiction in a book group or as a solitary activity has much to offer students and practitioners engaged in learning for practice. Drawing on these accounts, and my reflections regarding the effectiveness of these strategies as a means to progressing and consolidating understandings, what I offer here is the reading of fiction, whether individually or in groups, as a learning tool; an approach to knowledge acquisition that can be applied to a range of learning contexts for learners, practitioners and educators who are interested in innovative learning and teaching methods.

Key Points

Throughout the higher education experience and in post-qualifying development, the learner is expected to engage with literature, however in addition to academic style texts there is value in engaging with other texts, such as life stories and fictional texts. Readers can engage and reflect on the content alone but the coming together with others can lead to new insights and be a spur for deeper self and critical reflection.

- Engaging with novels and works of fiction can be a learning medium and teaching tool.
- The reading of literature can be utilised by students, practitioners, educators; individually or within a group.
- This chapter contextualises the pedagogy that underpins analytical reading in groups and individually.
- Book groups and the reading of fiction is a methodology that can be applied to inform the professional knowledge base.

Significance for Social Work Practice

An awareness of, and an openness to, the need to proactively engage with learning for practice, throughout the career trajectory, is the essence of professional development. Said learning can be accessed through a range of media and exists in countless guises. Yet it is the familiar methods of teaching and learning that are more likely to be employed and trusted, even though there are a number of less explicit, but equally as effective, approaches available (Triggs, 2015). Reading fiction in social work education is one of these and, until fairly recently, was an unexplored and underutilised learning activity diluted by a perception of reading as a conventional pastime (Hyder, 2013) devoid of relevance to a professional populace. This misinformed and problematic assumption is the reason why I draw attention to it, as book groups and the reading of fiction are not only feasible learning tools but ones that have incredible potential for realising development in social work education. As suggested earlier, the reading of fiction can be a solitary activity or engaged with within a group context – although the learning possibilities and reflective capacity is greater when engaging from within the group context. Either way, the main principles of the process rest within the purpose; a purpose driven by the learning requirements of those engaging with it and what they aim to achieve. Using this as a starting point we can begin to unpick the principles of the reading of fiction for practice and explore how it can be used as an accessible, diverse and flexible learning activity.

Stories are fundamental to life and living, they surround us and are accessed through listening to the accounts of others or through being conscious of the ones we create in our heads. They appear in different forms and are utilised in a variety of ways. There are those we craft to establish our dreams and aspirations, those we use when we need comfort and those that help us to make sense of the world. Pullman suggests that 'after nourishment, shelter and companionship, stories are the thing we need most in the world' (Pullman, 2011:74). Stories are often unexceptionally integral to human existence, but in essence impact, influence and shape our realities, offering extraordinary potential as we attempt to manage or maximise our lived experience. As Didion (cited in Taylor, 2015: 1) states, 'we tell ourselves stories in order to live'; and indeed we do. This is something that is particularly obvious if you think about the multilayered features of self-talk (Bandura, 2001) and how this strategy can be incredibly reassuring when we face adversity, or heartening when we are required to galvanise ourselves for some kind of action or other. Another way that we are exposed to stories is through the reading of literature, and it is through the engagement with these stories that we more often than not lose ourselves or are drawn in by a narrative as it unfolds. You only have to recall a memorable book you yourself have read, or listen to someone recount a piece of fiction to realise the powerful nature of story.

This process of storytelling can be likened to a social work exchange, where the service-user, as the narrator tells their story, and through active listening the practitioner reflects back the content in what should be a more digestible manner, in an attempt to create an environment that promotes change (Rogers, 2004). 'Telling stories is our way of coping, a way of creating shape out of a mess. It binds everyone together' (Polley in Kellaway, 2013:np).

Owing to this storytelling-type process (Egan, 2002) practitioners are able to analyse what has occurred, why it is occurring, and collate a chronology of events that have preceded a person, group or community presenting for assistance. The reading of fiction provides an opportunity to practise these and a range of other skills, but it does so in a more informal and ethical manner, given that it allows us to explore the story of fictional others. The scope of learning available within this activity encompasses the breadth of the professional requirements and standards for effective practice in that it creates a space to think, a time to reflect, an occasion to listen, a context to apply theory, and a backdrop in which to analyse what is occurring between the reader and the other as the story unfolds. It is a window through which the learner can look to enable them to explore the self in relation to the other and to process challenges and ethical dilemmas as they might arise. Choosing the right type of fiction is key to the effectiveness of this method and suggestions are offered below.

Using in Practice

Accessing fiction as a means to learning requires little more than the motivation to read, an interesting text and an enquiring mind. The genre should be carefully considered as it is this element of the planning that will determine the learning potential of the reading experience. The internet is an incredibly useful resource in this respect.

Using related words and terms, such as, 'book groups' or 'reading groups' in a search will provide a range of recommended texts, book reviews, with some websites going as far as suggesting questions to ask that are pertaining to various works. Autobiographies, novels, short stories, realistic fiction, the classics and journals are all useful to explore. It is important that readers and groups consider whether or not the text chosen provides content, characters and circumstances that are easily transferred into and contextualised from a social work perspective. Whether it is a sole activity or as part of a group, defining or redefining the purpose of the learning activity will assist with appropriateness of the book choice in the planning stage of the process. In addition, it will be helpful to list topics of interest, learning objectives and once agreed note the aims of reading from a particular text; subsequently linking all of this to practice and or professional development of the reader or group of readers.

Another layer of this learning activity is the method employed as readers weave through the pages of a text. Some learners might choose to read the text completely and then make some notes, others might make use of post-it type notes or annotate the text as they read, whereas others reading on electronic devices might use the notes and highlights features of this technology to record key themes, while there may be readers who do not feel it is necessary to record at all. This points to a very individual learning activity and one to be enjoyed through the flexibility it can offer. All that said there is one method that I would encourage and it is that of dialectical journaling, outlined further in Template 11.2. This is an annotative process that can be likened to both the gathering of information and analytical phases of a social work intervention; it is a critical commentary of the content or indeed a conversation with the text. Incorporating this type of practice into the learning event affords the reader with additional opportunities to pause and think, to ask questions of the text, and to reflect on what is occurring both within the pages and for the learner themselves. This recording activity can supplement the learning as it unfolds, as it is through journaling that the reader can further explain, question and rationalise the fictional content. By completing Template 11.1 the reading becomes more focused and purposeful. Structuring the reading within a framework elicits thinking that might otherwise get lost as readers are often drawn into one particular issue or a specific element of the story, which can impact on their ability to see the wider story. An example of this was notable at a recent social work book group, where we read The Children Act by Ian McEwan (2014). Each reader came to the group with pertinent points that they were keen to share and explore. Yet, what was most interesting were the reflections presented relating to the main character Fiona Maye, a High Court Judge. Some of the social work students, practitioners, researchers and academics, a fairly mixed group, had incredible empathy for Fiona and the circumstances she found herself in, some were quite ambivalent and then there were others who were unable to see anything other than her power and status. This one example highlights the individual nature of reading and indeed of the social work assessment, illustrating the significance of objectivity and highlighting the requirement to work within the internal reference of the other (Nelson-Jones, 1993).

> The only way we can know what is going on in the mind of someone who reads a story is to believe them when they tell us about it and compare it with our own experience of reading and see what we have in common. (Pullman, 2011:75)

A full live recording of the event discussed above can be accessed using this link: https://vls.uclan.ac.uk/Play/11058; this footage can be used as a learning resource as well as serving to outline a book group process. Thus, as we are beginning to see, book groups and the reading of fiction can enable learners to explore tensions as they arise – even more so when in the group context, as this example and the opening quotation to this part of the chapter suggests.

The pedagogy underpinning this reflective reading activity is based upon the Socratic methodology explained by Raider (2003:2) as 'the art or practice of examining opinions or ideas logically, often by the method of questions and answers, so as to determine their validity'. Individuals engage in dialogue to try to understand a text and this style of teaching and learning advocates critical thinking and is a method that aims to create and nurture questioning minds. Adler (1984) adds to our understanding of this methodology, explaining it as, 'asking questions, by leading discussions, by helping ... [individuals] to raise their minds up from a state of understanding and appreciating less to a state of understanding and appreciating more' (p.29). Here the learner is engaged as an active and equal partner (dialectic methodology) within the knowledge exchange, as opposed to the more traditional learner position of a passive recipient (didactic methodology), or the receiver of information (Vejar, 2008). It is possible to employ this method whether or not you choose to read within a group or alone. Put simply, you, as the reader, will have a conversation with the book through the journaling of your ideas and the scribing of issues as they arise. On conclusion, readers can then record learning and future learning needs as they reflect upon their professional development.

As remarked earlier, book groups provide an ethical space in which to learn, in that they remove the need to use actual case content, for learning, given that literature provides us with fictional characters and circumstances to reflect upon. Therefore, in this respect they address issues pertaining to confidentiality, as more often than not we refer to service-users' stories in learning spaces to help us to reflect and, inasmuch as this is necessary with regards to evidence-based practice, it is not something that the confines of confidentiality permits given that we do not seek consent that authorises the use of peoples' stories outside of the therapeutic exchange.

Tuning into the Work and the Social Work Process

Template 11.1 taken from Taylor (2014a: 45–46) is an aide memoire developed as a guide for learners, educators and book group facilitators that aims to capture the multi-dimensional layers of a social work assessment. This is a useful tool for a book group or the sole reader as it can be used as a prompt, element by element, or as a framework to reflect upon as the fictional text is read and discussed. However, there are no set patterns to this learning activity; as long as the reading process is accompanied by some level of analysis, application and reflection, which supports the professional development significant to the learner at that time.

Tuning-in, 'involves the worker's effort to get in touch with potential feelings and concerns that the client may bring to the helping encounter' and 'the technique can be employed before the contact … has begun' (Shulman, 1999: 44). The template offered here is a guide, prompt or outline, whichever is felt necessary by the reader or group, to provide some level of structure to the reading process. There is some value in having an outline of some description that can be referred to, as this adds focus and meaning to reading for learning in a social work context. This template can be adapted, revised or re-written to fit with the reader(s), the purpose or the environment where fiction is being employed as a tool for learning.

Template 11.1 Tuning into social work process

Referral: who has been referred, circumstance(s), the referral agent, documented category of the case.

Knowledge base: age, life stage, gender, perceived identity, family construct, social background, race, ethnicity, religion, spirituality, education, employment, (to include legislation and all set within a theoretical context); refer to Howe (2009).

Client group: pre-birth, children, adults, youth work, older adults, sensory, mental health, learning disability, physical disability, brain injury.

Practice setting: community, hospital, residential, education, health, day-care, criminal justice (statutory, voluntary or private agency).

Assessment approach: questioning, procedural, exchange; refer to Milner & O'Byrne (2002:53).

Method of intervention: outline the method of intervention: individual, group, family, community.

Practice approach: outline the practice approach (cognitive, behavioural, crisis, psychosocial, humanistic, task centred and rationale for the approach taken; include stages of the work (beginning, middle, and end).

Skills: which were employed, how did they work; refer to Trevithick (2005:82) skills inventory.

Value base: which were employed and why; refer to the origins of the professional value base (Biestek, 1957).

Care planning: outline the care planning process; refer to the classic text by Taylor & Devine (1993:41–69).

Implementation: approach taken to implementing the care plan; refer to the classic text by Taylor & Devine (1993:70–83).

Ethical dilemmas: outline any identified throughout the work and how these were addressed.

Evaluation: outcomes, what went well, what you might do differently next time, what have you learned?

Dialectical Journaling: Pedagogy and Practice

In higher education, journaling is also used as a tool to assist developing the reflective process as it is 'a crucible for processing the raw material of experience in order to integrate it with existing knowledge and create new meaning' (Kerka, 2002:1). Both the formation of book groups and the reading of fiction as a teaching methodology lend themselves to the aforementioned dialectical, otherwise known as the Socratic teaching and learning methodology. Carter and Gradin (2001) advocate the principle of using a dialectic notebook to record thoughts about what you are reading. Template 11.2 offers a framework for noting what you are commenting on within the text in a manner that enables one to capture a chronological analysis from a social work perspective. It is useful to get into the habit of making notes on the text, as one weaves through the pages, as a reminder of key points and as prompts to read further and to record responses pre and post the reflective element of the process – be that as a group and or as an individual learner.

Template 11.2 Dialectical journaling

Annotations	Main body of the fictional text	Reflections
Dialectical Journaling is an activity where the reader makes notes about the text, here, on the left hand margin of the book being read. The aim is to record thoughts, feelings or perceptions as they arise, or make comments on perceptions or themes as relevant, using the knowledge, values and skills framework as a guide. In essence, the reader, at this stage, is having a conversation with themselves about what is occurring within the text. Questions, themes and additional reading prompts can be recorded.		Reflections may be recorded during or after the reading phase, or when engaged in a Book Group discussion. Reflections can relate, again, to anything arising for the reader, relating to learning gleaned from engaging with the fictional content or the Book Group discussion. It can be a useful space to note further reading, new concepts, research or additional information that the reader might have learned or may wish to follow up. This again deepens the learning potential from engaging with the reading activity.

Here is the Dialectical Journaling template, which includes an example using an extract from Morgan's (2012) book Disappearing Home. Ten-year-old Robyn lives in a tenement block with her mother and abusive stepfather. Her unhappy childhood is punctuated by poverty and shoplifting.

Annotations	Main body of the fictional text	Reflections
Theory/Life Stages: Psychosocial theories of Human Development Mother – what has shaped behaviours and parenting style Father – the text gives some indication of indicators of parenting Robyn – how might she be feeling, is there normalisation in this narrative, or a lack of regard for the self – she is clearly at risk Themes/Issues arising: 1. Fear of what is occurring within the family home and dynamic (risks) 3. Impact of this experience on Robyn – multiple layers 4. How would I engage this family (method of intervention, skills and values)? 5. What am I feeling about all of this?	When they **first** sent me out to **steal** I was **ten years old**. The **bag bothered** me most. It was dirty on the outside as well as the inside. With brown leather handles that were frayed down to the white wire. They burned your skin if held for too long. Later, **they told me** I held it too high, like a bloody shield, and too far away from me when I walked with it. They said I held it like it was a disease. It's only soil. A bit of soil can be easily washed away. I was making it obvious. That was the last thing you did, make it obvious. That was **stupid** cos that's how you get caught and **if you get caught you're on your own**, you **stupid bitch**. *text in bold keywords underlined that shaped and influenced an analysis of what might be occurring *it might be helpful to go through this excerpt and identify words, phrases that stand out for you?	Follow up Professor Nicky Stanley's research – Domestic Violence Shaping influences/ Domains of Experience (Froggett 2002). Think more about systemic ways of understanding. Review research that discusses the interacting nature of the family on the individual lived experiences and how each attaches and influences the other? Notes from Book group: (recorded by the reader/learner) Or Learning points: (recorded by the reader/learner)

Recommended Reading List

Barham, P. (1997). *Closing The Asylum The Mental Patient in Modern Society*. London: Penguin Books.

Cherry, L. (2013). *The Brightness of Stars*. Oxfordshire: Wilson King Publishers.

Donoghue, E. (2010). *Room*. London: Picador Publishing.

Frankl, V. E. (2004). *Man's Search for Meaning*. London: Rider Publishers.

Masters, A. (2006). *Stuart – A Life Backwards*. London: Harper Perennial Publishing.

Morgan, D. (2012). *Disappearing Home*. Birmingham: Tindal Street Press.

McEwan, I. (2014). *The Children Act*. London: Jonathan Cape.

Peebles, S. (2013). *Snake Road*. London: Chatto & Windus Publisher.

Rogers, A. G. (1996). *Shining Affliction: A Story of Harm and Healing in Psychotherapy*. London: Penguin Books Ltd.

Rowling, J. K. (2013). *The Casual Vacancy*. London: The Little Brown Book Group.

Sapphire (1997). *Push*. New York: Knopft Doubleday Publishing Group.

Trigell, J. (2004). *Boy A*. London: Serpents Tail Publisher.

Winterson, J. (2012). *Why Be Happy When You Can Be Normal*. New York: Grove Press.

The choice of book will be individual to the reader and/or the group, set within the identified learning needs of each or both. The readings listed above offer a starting point for thinking about relevant and useful fiction. These texts have been utilised and subsequently recommended by various social work book groups in education and in practice settings. It is worthwhile noting that some groups, where time is of the essence, have chosen to read journal articles within the reading group context and have found this activity equally as satisfying from a learning perspective.

Conclusion

So, as we can see, fiction as a teaching and learning medium can help us to think through complex problems from a distanced position. It is a flexible, pleasurable and to a larger extent a self-directed experience, where we can engage as sole readers, or in groups. The environment, the book choice and the application of learning is at the discretion of the reader(s). Not only does it provide us with the opportunity to learn but it also affords us with time to contemplate and, if we so choose, to share these contemplations with peers through what is a type of group learning. Often it is through the perceptions of others that we can access deeper reflections, alternative insights and access realisations that we may not have had were it not for learning experiences such as these. It does all of this within a fictive space that creates an environment in which to delve into lives and circumstances in a way that is, to a larger extent, much more ethical in nature.

Interestingly, while reading the memoir of one of the most reputable social work scholars of our time, Olive Stevenson, I noted a brief account of her use of literature to support curriculum content in her teaching practice many years ago. Stevenson (2013) explains how she was 'fascinated by the dynamics and structure of drama and in general by the insight which literature throws on human relationships'. She goes on to detail how she 'initiated seminars for social work students using various forms of literature, including biography and novels' (p. 21). An account was retold through the lens of one of Professor Stevenson's students, June Thoburn, at a recent @SWBookGroup event (Taylor, 2014b). Professor Thoburn recited, with fondness, how her tutor would direct students to a fictional text that was to be read for class discussion and also how she would walk them to various places in the local community to facilitate yet another level of awareness of 'other' in context (Klein, 1997).

Until this point I was largely unaware of any formal use of fiction as a vehicle for learning in social work education, but as a result of developing a national book group, found that it has and is being used by some academics and educators in a more informal and ad hoc manner. It is my hope, one I stumbled over while teaching some incredibly astute students, for whom literature and fiction was a mainstay of their existence, that like for them and now for me, this learning context can become a lens through which practitioners, both present and future, can further access understandings as they continue to navigate the complexities of social work practice.

You can find Social Work Book Group online @SWBookGroup and are welcome to join what is becoming a global 'community of learning for practice' (Wenger, 2000).

12
Social Work Narratives: My Learning Journey

Sue Gardner, Heidi Harbin, Amanda Murphy and Susan Woods

Sue Gardner: Newly Qualified Social Worker

In this reflective narrative I share with the reader some of my experiences in undertaking a BA Hons Social Work degree and the subsequent transition from social work education into the role of newly qualified practitioner, embarking on my Assessed and Supported Year in Employment (ASYE).

The motivation to work with children and families through the medium of social work arose through a life-changing personal experience involving the loss of a family member and coming into contact with many different professionals and service users. However, reflecting as I write, I understand from the learning that took place over my three-year degree course, that it could be argued the journey to become a social worker began many years before, with the separation of my parents and sibling group at a very early age. What my life experiences stirred in me was a strong desire to build a career that had the potential to make a difference to other children and their families and social work seemed like the perfect choice. What I didn't expect was to be faced with physical and emotional barriers when entering into the education stream of social work practice, and how difficult it would be to overcome them. Cross (1992) identifies three barriers – Situational, Institutional and Dispositional and these resonated deeply with my feelings at that time. Factors like finances, family responsibilities and student debt all needed to be considered; however the biggest barrier of all was my own confidence to achieve success in an academic environment when in my mid-to-late 30s. Cross (1992) discusses the stigma attached to admitting such doubts and that as the first two barriers are overcome, then dispositional barriers have to be faced.

A pivotal moment in my student social work studies involved Psychosocial Studies, the module I was least looking forward to, in all honesty. I remember studying theorists such as Erikson, Freud and Klein and thinking they could be speaking in another language, due to my lack of understanding. Persisting with the subject, it eventually came together in an essay structured around applying the learnt concepts to your own narrative and to the service users worked with in placement. This created an opportunity for a shift in perspective, which changed my understanding of many personal life events and the key people involved in them. Importantly, it also brought to life a book recommended to me by my personal tutor, Howe's *The Emotionally Intelligent Social Worker* (2008). Howe discusses the emotions/feelings that are present in all our social interactions. Many service users experience poverty, disadvantage, loss, illness etc. and these circumstances lead to levels of emotions which are often stressfully aroused and behaviours which are inextricably linked (Howe, 2008). Having a clearer understanding of the emotional responses of the people I work with, as well as those felt by me, has undoubtedly helped me to become a more mindful and effective practitioner.

Graduating with a First Class Social Work Honours Degree opened some unexpected doors. The opportunity to study at postgraduate level warred with my need to gain much needed practice experience, and regain financial stability. In the end I tried to do both, deciding to enrol in a part-time postgraduate (evening) course while securing full-time employment. Discussing employment options with my personal tutor gave me the confidence to apply my studies to the interview process and the service user group I hoped to work with. The majority of my academic work and my final placement had centred around the lives of Children Looked-After (CLA) whereas Child Protection roles were the main vacancies available and seemed an inevitable employment route. However, a voluntary sector agency (that coincidentally provided my first placement) was recruiting for an Adoption Social Worker. I made contact with them and was informed that a minimum of two years' experience was required – however I was welcome to apply regardless! To my surprise I was offered an interview and spent the next two weeks digesting every bit of adoption policy, legislation, current CLA statistics and agency history/values that I could source.

I believe it was those values the agency represented that were key to me and another NQSW being offered positions with that agency. They departed from their more traditional stance of employing experienced workers and engaged wholeheartedly with supporting and upholding the principles of ASYE. My first year was guided and fully supported not only by my supervisor, but all my colleagues around me. Those supportive relationships have been key to my continuing development of knowledge and skills, in what proved to be one of the busiest years in the adoption team, and my ability to succeed in this environment. Working with dedicated social workers – who, although busy, always found time for me – and sharing their knowledge and values is everything I hoped for in my working life but truly didn't think I would be able to find in the current pressurised climate of social work practice.

The role of an adoption social worker is highly emotive and a position that I find holds huge responsibilities; we are making decisions which affect a life time, not just a moment. Smith (2008: 5) discussed the role of power and states: 'Social work interventions are likely to have a profound effect on people's lives.' To continue to practise, and to be resilient and remain effective, I have had to use supervision to work through these complex issues and feelings, as do my more experienced colleagues. I believe good supervision is a much-needed foundation in any good social work practice and I am thankful that my agency engages in regular formal and informal supervision. My experience of supervision has not fallen short of the ideal advocated by Kadushin and Harkness (2014) but I am aware that others have less favourable experiences outside of my own agency (Kadushin & Harkness, 2014).

Having just completed my second year in social work, I have no regrets about my career choice; it saddens me to hear of colleagues who have already left the profession. I am concerned about the future of social work, with the incorporation of schemes such as Frontline, which involve dramatically reduced academic learning. While I accept that there is always room for improvement and change, I feel strongly about the time needed to develop as a student social worker and the necessity for good quality student placements and a fit for purpose ASYE, which employers have the commitment and resources to uphold for NQSWs, believing this will secure the quality and resilience of workers in such a demanding environment.

Heidi Harbin: Senior Social Worker and Best Interest Assessor

Nineteen years after embarking upon a diploma in social work, I find myself working as a best interest assessor/senior practitioner for Bolton Council. I do a job I enjoy and feel the role is valuable and challenging. The journey to this point has not been planned. The course of my social work career has been inevitably shaped by ever changing statutory duties, opportunities that arise from service re-developments and working with colleagues and managers that are able to inspire. The learning context in which social workers practise is important to acknowledge, however, as an individual there needs to be an openness to continue learning and to take opportunities as they arise.

In 1996, upon completion of a psychology degree, the next apparently obvious step was to commence a career within that field. Competition to study clinical psychology at that time was fierce so, following a rejection from that course, I needed to rethink my options. I had always had an interest in mental health, and thought social work would be another route into working in that field.

The diploma in social work took two years to complete. Over the duration of the course my perspective of what social work was developed, and it has not stopped developing since. Upon qualifying I worked as a hospital social worker, assessing the needs of adults in a hospital environment and setting up care packages – the whole care management process that was the NHS and Community Care Act 1990. On the induction week every person I met (from occupational therapists to home care managers) appeared to be saying they 'assess and meet needs' and I was unsure what made social workers any different.

It didn't take long to understand the value that social workers brought to the assessment processes. It was here that I understood the worth of social work values, and how putting these into practice and challenging medical models was so vital to the experience of people involved in the system. Of course I learnt how to become an administrator of the local authority's scarce resources, but attempted to do so in an empowering and person-centred manner.

After three months at the hospital, I got a job on an area social work team, working with older adults. In the busy hospital, team individuals welcomed my presence as I was setting up packages of care to enable patients to be discharged as soon as possible.

However, in the community I found myself involved in safeguarding investigations and visiting people in their own homes who really did not want me to be there. My colleagues on the team appeared immensely knowledgeable and skilled and it felt like a whole new role. Here I realised the importance of learning from your peers. Discussing cases with your peers is not a sign of weakness; rather, it enables a healthy working environment, better reflection on the options and ultimately a better outcome for the service users. This felt like being in a team.

While in this team I was asked by the manager to clarify the local authority's duties to foreign nationals with no leave to remain in the country and this involved liaison with the legal department and researching duties in the National Assistance Act 1948. It was at this point that I realised still further what made social work different to other professionals involved in assessments. The law explicitly underpins all our actions and informs what we should do, what we may do and how this is interpreted in practice. After practising social work for two years the elements which defined social work became clearer to me.

My interest in the statutory role of social workers led to my becoming an Approved Social Worker. This involved a placement in a mental health team and completion of accredited university modules. An opportunity arose for a position in a Community Mental Health Team for older people and I commenced working in a team of social workers, psychiatric nurses and an occupational therapist. This was in the early days of multi-disciplinary working; on arrival in the team the nurses and social workers even had separate tea funds. Breaking down the barriers between health and social care professionals was enabled by utilising interpersonal skills. It was necessary to challenge the stereotypes that were in place relating to how health and social professionals were perceived. It didn't take long to develop good working relationships within the team, emphasising the positive aspects of each profession and acknowledging that, ultimately, we all shared the same goal in relation to the outcome for service users.

Changes in my own circumstances led to a move away from the unpredictability of the approved social work rota and I became a senior practitioner in an adults' assessment team. This role provided me with a new challenge. Mentoring, consultation and joint working cases enabled me to critically reflect on my own practice.

Changes in the law in 2009 led to the creation of the Best Interest Assessor role in applying the Deprivation of Liberty Safeguards. The statutory nature of the role requires understanding, interpretation and application of the law and I received specialist training through an accredited university module. At the time I did the training I did not anticipate that case law would create an explosion in the number of requests for authorisations. An opportunity arose to be a best interest assessor in the council, which is my current role. Recent proposals from the Law Commission are likely to impact on this role in the next two to three years, with the potential creation of an Approved Mental Capacity Professional (AMCP) role. This may be a future opportunity, or service redevelopments may offer alternative challenges.

Completing the Diploma in Social Work gave me the basic skills to practise as a social worker. The competencies that needed to be met for the diploma are still as relevant today as they were 19 years ago. For instance, to be able to communicate and engage, to promote and enable, are vital to all social work practice, whether working with service users, colleagues or other professionals. The knowledge necessary to be a competent social worker comes from academic learning and experience. To learn from your experience and be flexible in light of changing circumstances necessitates a pragmatic approach to career development.

Amanda Murphy: Independent Social Worker and Approved Mental Health Professional, and Former Principal Social Worker

Beginning to describe my journey into social work with a confession probably isn't the expected approach; but I can't deny the fact that I never intended to be a social worker and didn't start out with it as my number one career! There, I've said it, and it actually feels rather good to come clean. But now let me properly explain. As a 16-year-old college student with an interest in psychology and commitment to spending my summers volunteering at local charitable mental health day centres, I think it's only fair to say that the school careers adviser had fully drawn a blank in being able offer any constructive advice and helpfully signposted me to a computer where I could answer random questions in the hope of producing a golden ticket leading me down the career path of merriment. I told it I was interested in people, society and independence and that I wanted to work in the community; 'be an Occupational Therapist' it said. 'OK' I said, and off I went.

As a child I remember wanting to be a Missionary Worker having overheard a conversation between my mother and aunt, but as religion and I didn't quite see eye to eye it was never really going to gather any momentum; but I was curious about people and often spoke out when I felt people were not being listened to or were being taken advantage of – and usually to my own detriment!

But, the computer had spoken. I chose my A Levels in accordance with Occupational Therapy requirements with the aim of applying to university and securing a job in mental health (which had become my main interest and motivation following an experience of a family member). But after exposure to Occupational Therapists in practice through my voluntary work, I decided it wasn't for me. While I observed a definite focus on independence, there was something missing about the need to understand a person within their world, the importance of relationships and the systems we find ourselves in. And so I returned to the drawing board with very little direction.

University came around and by this point I had decided that a career in Social Work was much more suited to the 'things' I held dear – things such as social justice, challenging inequality, promoting independence, being anti-discriminatory and anti-oppressive – 'things' I now know to be core to the Social Work profession. But being 18 years old in 1996 meant that I was too young to apply directly and so getting a degree while waiting to grow older and continuing with my voluntary work seemed to be the only other option. Part way through my Philosophy and Cultural Studies degree I grew impatient and took myself off to the School of Social Work and spoke with a kindly Senior Lecturer, passionately telling him about out why I wanted to be a social worker. Shortly afterwards I sat an entrance exam and the rest, as they say, is history. I qualified with a Diploma in Social Work in 1999 having had two placements in mental health settings which were utterly enlightening and only confirmed that this was the right path for me.

Having secured a role in a community mental health team I quickly became interested in the relationship between social factors and mental illness and the Social Work role within. This encouraged me to complete a postgraduate diploma in effective community care for people with mental health problems; an evidence-based approach which complimented my developing Social Work skills and interventions. From here I moved into an Assertive Outreach team whose model and philosophy completely chimed with my understanding of Social Work practice; based on models founded in the US, Assertive Outreach teams involved small, multidisciplinary teams focusing upon 'home-based crisis intervention … coping skills, meaningful roles and meaningful relationships, including family support' (Rosen, 1992: 258). Here I felt able to really contribute to a person's overall well-being and best utilise my Social Work interventions; the impact on outcomes for service users, who had struggled with repeated and lengthy admissions to hospital, was significant and the value of social perspectives and evidence-based practice brought by me as the teams' Social Worker was very much acknowledged.

Over the past 16 years I have been fortunate enough to have experienced a varied career, having worked in community-based mental health teams and a mental health day hospital, supported a number of Social Work students through their practice placements, qualified as an Approved Social Worker (latterly Approved Mental Health Professional), a Team Manager, a Learning and Development Lead, the lead for Approved Mental Health Professionals and then Principal Social Worker; all of which I think is testament to the Social Work role and its 'transferability'.

There are many proud moments over my career, from seeing service users transform their lives to a place where they feel a sense of achievement, to joint working with universities to facilitate fantastic practitioner-focused events, to guiding social workers through complex cases and seeing their knowledge grow, to managing a whole service transformation and being comforted when little goes wrong! Social workers are skilled practitioners but sometimes among all the business, we forget to stop and reflect, we overlook our abilities and miss out on celebrating our own successes.

However, I can't say that it hasn't been without its challenges! It is well documented that social workers in the early days of the integrated mental health team felt that their once clearly-defined role had become blurred with that of their health colleagues and that being managed by non-Social Work professionals posed a challenge to their professional standpoint. I completely identified with this as, while integration offered a number of opportunities, it also brought with it a loss of identity. A Social Work student once asked me how

I kept hold of what it was to be a social worker despite the changing landscape, and I really had to think for a moment. But essentially I decided that it was about standing firm to Social Work values and applying Social Work theory to practice; because sometimes it isn't that you are performing a different task, but it's how you perform that task which will stand you apart from other professionals and enable you to retain clarity in your casework.

There have been a few tools which have proven essential to my practice over the years, and the function of professional supervision has been the most important; and not just while in front-line practice. Prioritising the space to pause and explore complexities, challenges and approaches has enabled me to develop confidence and competence in my practice and to enable me to keep going when times have been tough. Seeking out like-minded professionals, regardless of their professional background was another invaluable source of professional support, providing vital peer support and leading to greater understanding and clarity of roles when working within integrated services.

There are constantly changing times in the world of social care, what with the introduction of the Care Act and the ongoing review of Mental Capacity and Deprivation of Liberty Safeguards by the Law Commission, yet I remain positive about the future of Social Work, believing it to be a strong profession which is only boosted by social care legislation. And having now taken the plunge into Independent Practice, I feel positive about my own future and excited to see where my knowledge and skills will take me.

Susan Woods: Retired Social Worker and Independent Reviewing Officer Specialising in Child Protection Plans and Care Plans for Looked-After Children

My journey into social work, specifically children and families, probably began, unbeknown to me, when I was a child. My mother, I later found out, developed a paranoid schizophrenic illness brought on by neglected puerperal psychosis after my birth. This was the 1950s and I spent my childhood hiding the secret from friends and protecting my father, who was unable to understand such behaviour as an illness, viewing it as 'bad blood' or 'instability'.

During my early days of practice I began to think that most people came into social work in one of three ways: either through their religious belief, through political convictions or through childhood difficulties. Since the 1990s this has been much less apparent – and I don't know if this is good or bad. As a vocational profession like teaching and nursing, I still feel it is crucial to one's social work practice to understand what drives you to want to make a difference, as this can affect your judgements and your prejudices. I was certainly a 'rescuer' and this has affected my ability to delegate and my need to achieve outcomes.

This was my first important lesson: you cannot make people better, or always protect everyone. Human beings have to develop their own motivation to change. Having a manager who can help you explore such inner drivers and help you to prioritise personal and professional development with space to reflect on your practice is very important in such complex work. At the same time a manager also needs to be firm and clear about the need to protect yourself while understanding the requirement to follow procedures, all the while recording and evidencing your decisions.

I commenced my career as a primary school teacher, working in schools serving deprived areas in Blackpool. I quickly found I was more concerned with the background of the children and how this impacted on their behaviour, presentation and ability to learn. When the opportunity arose to go into social work, I took it and became an assistant social worker on a team working with elderly and/or physically disabled people. Qualifying as a social worker in 1984 I moved into generic social work, where I found practice was dominated by child protection and mental health work. I undertook mental health approved social work training and as my next job was as a child protection specialist, I undertook a postgraduate training course in Child Protection at Lancaster University. I later completed my practice teacher training. These three advanced training courses in different aspects of social work broadened my practice substantially. The next part of my journey was as a manager in children's services, finally becoming an Independent Reviewing Officer, reviewing child protection plans and care plans for Looked-After Children.

My teaching background gave me two important skills, which I have found invaluable throughout my childcare practice: a thorough understanding of child development and psychology; and an ability to work directly and communicate with children. I learnt early on that I had to have a job where I remained in touch with the primary service users, that is, children and their parents. Higher or middle management, with its endless political, strategic meetings, was not for me. Maybe I needed to be a backbencher in the political sense, someone who could criticise without ever being in a position of power to change things. That is why the job of independent reviewing officer was perfect for me. I could influence and affect decisions being made for individual children without becoming involved in the political and strategic arena. There was room to be imaginative in my advice and approaches to working with children and families in order to achieve the best outcomes, as the role had a level of independence from the Local Authority social work teams.

I didn't have an induction plan when I started my career in social work – the 'in at the deep end', 'sink or swim' theory was in vogue. I now recognise the importance of a comprehensive induction period. I have seen the importance of social workers building up their knowledge of community resources, not just professional referral points but what is universally available for service users.

Having worked for three Local Authorities has helped me to see that there are different strategic ways of meeting service users' needs. Training opportunities have proved vital to my own development. I have come away from the majority of training events I have attended feeling inspired and rejuvenated. Having experienced generic practice and having been fortunate to work in the days when social workers from all disciplines were part of the same area, I developed a much more sophisticated and deeper understanding of human problems across the lifecourse.

Finally the support of colleagues within a team and the humour that develops and carries you through the stress of this work has proven invaluable for me. Paying attention to the role of team dynamics has been vital and is particularly significant in current social work practice where so many social workers no longer have their own personal office space and desk.

Conclusion

Clare Stone and Fiona Harbin

We hope that you have found this book both informative and useful regardless of where you are along your professional learning journey. In writing this book we aimed to speak to social workers, students, educators and supervisors to promote key messages about learning and developing the professional self. Through our experiences as social workers and educators we recognise the amazing work that practitioners do on a daily basis and feel saddened that the profession is lambasted at every turn. Despite changes to initial training and an ever increasing regulation, a discourse of failure has endured within social work for over four decades. The ongoing criticism from the media and within the political arena illustrates to us the lack of understanding about the difference between initial education and the need to support ongoing continued professional development. In the introduction we used a tree as a metaphor to explain our conceptualisation of the difference between competence to pass a qualifying social work programme and the need to engage in career-long learning.

Social work employers can support the practitioner in their development by providing high quality reflective supervision and structured developmental programmes during the first year of practice (and ideally beyond), and facilitate opportunities to engage with a wide range of training and learning opportunities. Within the chapters we have provided insight into how employers, managers, practice educators and supervisors can support social worker development and have offered theories and tools to draw upon within practice. We encourage individuals to make full use of the support afforded to them, however we give a strong message within the text that individuals must take responsibility for their own learning and development.

Even when learning opportunities are given to social workers, they will not necessarily learn if they have not engaged with the learning ethos. We therefore ask that learners think about not only their own learning needs in terms of what needs to be learnt, but also consider the how of learning. Learners need to think about what works best for them and actively seek out support. Social workers must be motivated to take responsibility for learning throughout their careers and actively engage in the learning package. We situate reflective practice as important for adult learners and use the reflective principle throughout the book. Regardless of what the experience and activity is, we ask that the social worker think about it beforehand to draw upon existing knowledge, skills and values to help them prepare. During the event there is opportunity to be intuitive and responsive and as we become more experienced we further develop this ability, which is often referred to as practice wisdom. Reflecting after the event is essential to celebrate the strengths and identify the aspects of self and practice that can be improved upon. However this cognitive activity is a waste of time unless you do something with the new insights gained. Consider how you can replicate those things that went well and devise a plan of action for those aspects which need working on.

Whether you have read specific chapters or read the book in its entirety you will see the principles of reflective practice both explicitly and implicitly woven throughout this text. The exercises and tools ask that you think about yourself or your practice in depth, in order to generate insight but always with a view to self-improvement or improving practice. We believe that to maintain your ability to be a safe and effective practitioner you need to be reflective, prepared to learn new things and fine-tune existing skills, values and knowledge. In addition to thinking about the practitioner self in isolated terms we remind you to look beyond the self to think in a more critical way to explore how wider aspects impact upon practice. Consider the power at play, legislation and structures that shape and limit practice.

The journey of self and critical reflection for professional development starts within the university setting and must continue throughout your career. Reflecting upon the self is not easy – it takes time, it is exposing and it can make you feel vulnerable. Motivation is therefore essential to explore the self and keep going despite the setbacks and challenges along the way. Some of you will prefer to reflect alone but there is value in working with a trusted other. A peer, educator or supervisor can help create a safe and supportive space and importantly they can offer alternative perspectives, can challenge and can provide constructive feedback. The value of working with another in this way has been explored in terms of developing aspects of self, such as becoming an adult learner, developing emotional intelligence and resilience for practice. The chapters on supervision and coaching of course explore the importance of learning through supportive learning relationships. However the chapters on digitalisation and engaging with literature invite us to consider extending our learning relationships across different networks both physically and virtually. We can also learn a great deal about our professional attributes and practice by hearing and valuing the voice of those who use social work services. Chapter 9, co-written by representatives from a service user and career centre draws attention to learning about and learning from service users.

We are delighted to include within our book narratives from a range of social workers who are at different stages of their careers. The brief we gave them was certainly brief as we merely asked them to reflect upon the value of learning within their social work journey. We had no idea what they would write so we were therefore elated with their contributions because of the manner in which their stories resonate with the principles we advocate in this book. Their reflections tell of the value of learning and attending to professional development. It is interesting to note the twists and turns within their career trajectories and the commonality of their opinion in relation to the need to keep abreast of changes to practice, legislation and within their areas of responsibility. These social workers recognise the benefits of ongoing career-long learning and reflection upon the self for effective and safe practice.

We hope that you have enjoyed reading this book and find value in the exercises and content. We wish you well in your transformative learning journey.

Bibliography

Adler, M. J. (1984). *The Paideia Program: An Educational Manifesto*. New York: Collier Books, Macmillan Publishing Company.
Angelou, M. (2004). *Collected Autobiographies of Maya Angelou: I Know Why the Caged Bird Sings*. Westminster, MD: Random House.
Baim, C. & Guthrie, L. (2014). *Changing Offending Behaviour*. London: Jessica Kingsley Publishers.
Baim, C. & Morrison, T. (2011). *Attachment-based Practice with Adults*. Hove: Pavilion.
Baker, S., Warburton, J., Hodgkin, S. & Pascal, J. (2014). 'Reimagining the Relationship Between Social Work and Information Communication Technology in the Network Society', *Australian Social Work*, vol. 67, no. 4, pp. 467–478.
Bandura, A. (2001). 'Social Cognitive Theory: An Agentic Perspective', *Annual Review of Psychology*, vol. 52, pp. 1–26.
Barham, P. (1997). *Closing The Asylum: The Mental Patient in Modern Society*. London: Penguin Books.
Barnes, M. & Cotterell, P. (eds) (2012). *Critical Perspectives on User Involvement* [electronic resource]. Bristol: The Policy Press, p. 201.
Barretti, M. A. (2007). 'Teachers and Field Instructors as Student Role Models: A Neglected Dimension in Social Work Education', *Journal of Teaching in Social Work*, vol. 27, no. 3–4, pp. 215–239.
BASW (2012). *Social Media Policy*. http://cdn.basw.co.uk/upload/basw_34634-1.pdf, date accessed 1 May 2015.
BASW (2014). 'Stress and Too Tight Caseloads Cited as Reasons to Quit the Profession', *Professional Social Work*, November.
Bates, N., Immins, T., Parker, J., Keen, S., Rutter, L., Brown, K. & Zsigo, S. (2010). '"Baptism of Fire": The First Year in the Life of a Newly Qualified Social Worker', *Social Work Education*, vol. 29, no. 2.
BDO (2012). From Housing and Litter to Facebook and Twitter. http://www.bdo.co.uk/__data/assets/pdf_file/0008/186524/BDO_Local_Government_Team_-_Updating_your_status_social_media_report.pdf, date accessed 1 May 2015.
BDO (2013). Following the Trends. Results from the 2013 BDO Local Government Social Media Survey – today's trends and making the most of the medium. http://www.bdo.co.uk/__data/assets/pdf_file/0009/186525/following_the_trends_2013.pdf, date accessed 1 May 2015.

Beddoe, L., Davys, A. M. & Adamson, C. (2014). '"Never Trust Anybody Who Says 'I Don't Need Supervision'": Practitioners' Beliefs about Social Worker Resilience', *Practice* (09503153), vol. 26, no. 2, pp. 113–130.

Bellinger, A. (2010). 'Talking about (Re)Generation: Practice Learning as a Site of Renewal for Social Work', *British Journal of Social Work*, vol. 40, no. 8, pp. 2450–2466.

Belshaw, D. (2014). The Essential Elements of Digital Literacies. Self-published pdf. http://digitalliteraci.es, date accessed 10 June 2015.

Beresford, P. (2012). 'The Theory and Philosophy Behind User Involvement', in P. Beresford & S. Carr (eds), *Social Care, Service Users and User Involvement: Research Highlights in Social Work 55*. London: Jessica Kingsley Publishers.

Beresford, P. (2013). *Beyond the Usual Suspects. Towards Inclusive User Involvement. A Practical Guide*. http://www.shapingourlives.org.uk/documents/BTUSGUIDE.pdf, accessed on June 2014.

Berry-Lound, D. & Rowe, V. (2013). *Evaluation of the Implementation of the Assessed and Supported Year in Employment (the ASYE) for Skills for Care*. West Sussex: HOST Policy Research.

Biestek, F. P. (1957). *The Casework Relationship*. London: George Allen and Unwin.

Biggs, J. (1996). 'Enhancing Teaching Through Constructive Alignment', *Higher Education*, no. 3, 347.

Biggs, J. & Tang, C. (2007). *Teaching for Quality Learning at University: What the Student Does* (3rd edn). Buckingham: Open University Press.

Bleakley, A. (2005). 'Stories as Data, Data as Stories: Making Sense of Narrative Inquiry in Clinical Education', *Medical Education*, vol. 39, pp. 534–540.

Bogg, D. & Challis, M. (2013). *Evidencing CPD. A Guide To Building Your Social Work Portfolio*. St Albans: Critical Publishing.

Bogo, M., Regehr, C., Woodford, M., Hughes, J., Power, R. & Regehr, G. (2006). 'Beyond Competencies: Field Instructors' Descriptions of Student Performance', *Journal of Social Work Education*, vol. 42, no. 3, pp. 579–593.

Boyd, D. M. & Ellison, N. B. (2007). 'Social Network Sites: Definition, History and Scholarship', *Journal of Computer-Mediated Communication*, vol. 13, no. 1, pp. 210–230.

Branfield, F. (2009). *Developing User Involvement in Social Work Education*. http://www.shapingourlives.org.uk/resources/our-resources/all-publications/developing-user-involvement-in-social-work-education-2009, date accessed 1 May 2015.

Brookfield, S. (2009). 'The Concept of Critical Reflection: Promises and Contradictions', *European Journal of Social Work*, vol. 12, no. 3, pp. 293–304.

Brown, K., Skeen, L. M., Gray, I., Parker, J. & Gilpin, D. (2009). *Newly Qualified Social Workers: A Handbook for Practice*. Exeter: Learning Matters.
Care Act 2014 (2014). http://www.legislation.gov.uk/ukpga/2014/23/pdfs/ukpga_20140023_en.pdf, date accessed 1 May 2015.
Care Council for Wales (2015). *Practice Guidance for Social Workers*. http://www.ccwales.org.uk/practice-guidance-for-social-workers/, date accessed 1 May 2015.
Carpenter, J., Shardlow, S. M., Patsios, D. & Wood, M. (2015). 'Developing the Confidence and Competence of Newly Qualified Child and Family Social Workers in England: Outcomes of a National Programme', *British Journal of Social Work*, vol. 45, no. 1, pp. 153–176.
Carpenter, J., Webb, C., Bostock, L. & Coomber, C. (2012). *SCIE Research Briefing 43: Effective Supervision in Social Work and Social Care*. London: SCIE.
Carson, E., King, S. & Papatraianou, L. H. (2011). Resilience Among Social Workers: The Role of Informal Learning in the Workplace. *Practice* (09503153), vol. 23, no. 5, pp. 267–278.
Carter, D. & Gradin, S. (2001). *Writing as Reflective Action: A Reader*. New York: Longman Pearson.
Cassidy, S. (2010). 'Learning Styles: An Overview of Theories, Models, and Measures', *Educational Psychology*, vol. 24, no. 4, pp. 419–444.
Chambers, A. (2012). *Student Physiotherapists' Narratives and the Construction of Professional Identities*. A thesis submitted to the School of Education, University of Manchester for the Degree of Doctorate in Education in the Faculty of Humanities.
Cherry, L. (2013). *The Brightness of Stars*. Oxfordshire: Wilson King Publishers.
Clapton, G. (2013). 'Ideas in Action: Minding the Gap: Assisting the Transition from the Academy to the Profession,' *Social Work Education*, vol. 32, no. 3, pp. 411–415.
Collins, S. (2007). 'Social Workers, Resilience, Positive Emotions and Optimism', *Practice: Social Work in Action*, vol. 19, no. 4, pp. 255–269.
Collins, S. (2015). 'Alternative Psychological Approaches for Social Workers and Social Work Students Dealing with Stress in the UK: Sense of Coherence, Challenge Appraisals, Self-Efficacy and Sense of Control', *British Journal of Social Work*, vol. 45, no. 1, 69–85.
Cotton, J. (1995). *The Theory of Learning: An Introduction*. London: Kogan Page.
Cross, K. P. (1992) *Adults as Learners: Increasing Participation and Facilitating Learning* (1st edn). San Francisco: Jossey-Bass.
CWDC (2010). *Guide for Supervisors, Newly Qualified Social Worker Pilot Programme 2008–2009*. London: UCL.
Dacre Pool, L., Qualter, P. & Sewell, P. (2014). 'Exploring the Factor Structure of the CareerEDGE Employability Development Profile', *Education + Training*, vol. 56, no. 4, pp. 303–313.

Dalzell, R. & Sawyer, E. (2007). 'Putting Analysis into Assessment: Undertaking Assessments of Need – A Toolkit for Practitioners', *National Children's Bureau*.

de las Olas Palma-García, M. & Hombrados-Mendieta, I. (2014). 'The Development of Resilience in Social Work Students and Professionals', *Journal of Social Work*, vol.14, no. 4, pp. 380–397.

Department for Education (DFE) & Skills for Care (SFC). (no date). Resource 1: Seeking feedback from people who need care and support. *ASYE 7: Feedback from People Supported by NQSWs*.

Dickens, J. (2011). 'Social Work in England at a Watershed – as always: From the Seebohm Report to the Social Work Task Force', *British Journal of Social Work*, vol. 41, no. 1, pp. 22–39.

DiClemente, C. C. & Prochaska, J. O. (1982). 'Transtheoretical Therapy: Toward a More Integrative Model of Change', *Journal of Consulting and Clinical Psychology*, vol. 5, pp. 390–395.

DiNucci, D. (1999). 'Fragmented Future'. Print 53: 32. http://darcyd.com/fragmented_future.pdf, date accessed 1 May 2015.

Doel, M. & Shardlow, S. (1993). 'Examination by Triangulation: A Model for Practice Teaching', *Social Work Education*, vol. 12, no. 3, pp. 67–79.

Donoghue, E. (2010). *Room*. London: Picador Publishing.

Douglas, H. (2008). 'Preparation for Contact: An Aid to Effective Social Work Intervention', *Social Work Education*, vol. 27, no. 4, pp. 380–389.

Egan, G. (2002). *The Skilled Helper: A Problem Management and Opportunity Development Approach to Helping* (7th edn). Pacific Grove CA: Brooks Cole.

Ellingsen, I. T., Størksen, I. & Stephens, P. (2010). 'Q Methodology in Social Work Research', *International Journal of Social Research Methodology: Theory & Practice*, vol. 13, no. 5, pp. 395–409.

Ellis, J. (2003, June). *Socratic Seminars: Creating a Community of Inquiry*. In Socratic Method: Dialectic and Its Use in Teaching Culture in EFL Classrooms. Servet Çelik. Issue (5), http://www.greecesd.org/files/filesystem/GRTCN_Socratic_Seminars.pdf, date accessed 22 February 2015.

Engelberg, E. & Sjoberg, L. (2005). 'Emotional Intelligence and Interpersonal skills', in R. Schulze & R. D. Roberts (eds), *Emotional Intelligence: An International Handbook*. Cambridge: Hogrefe and Huber.

Eraut, M. (1998). 'Concepts of Competence', *Journal of Interprofessional Care*, vol. 12, no. 2, pp. 127–139.

Fang, L., Mishna, F., Zhang V. F., Van Wert, M. & Bogo, M. (2014). 'Social Media and Social Work Education: Understanding and Dealing with the New Digital World', Social Work in Health Care, 53:9, 800-814, DOI: 10.1080/00981389.2014.943455.

Gillespie, E. (2013) Sustainable storytelling is a powerful tool that communicates vision. *The Guardian* [online] 28 January. Available at: http://www.theguardian.com/sustainable-business/blog/sustainable-stories-powerful-tool-communicates-vision [Accessed 03 February 2013].

Fleming, J. (2012). 'Service User Involvement – What it is and what it could be. Lessons from the standards we expect project', in P. Beresford & S. Carr (eds), *Social Care, Service Users and User Involvement*. London: Jessica Kingsley Publisher.

Fook, J. (2012). *Social Work. A Critical Approach to Practice*. London: SAGE.

Fook, J. & Gardner, F. (2007). *Practising Critical Reflection: A Resource Handbook*. Maidenhead: Open University Press.

Forehand, M. (2012). *Bloom's Taxonomy. From Emerging Perspectives on Learning, Teaching and Technology*, http://epltt.coe.uga.edu/index.php?title=Bloom%27s_Taxonomy, date accessed 1 May 2015.

Frank, A. (2007). *The Diary of Anne Frank*. London: Puffin.

Frankl, V. E. (2004). *Man's Search for Meaning*. London: Rider Publishers.

Froggett, L. (2002). *Love, Hate and Welfare: Psychosocial Approaches to Policy and Practice*. Bristol, UK: The Policy Press.

Fursland, E. (2014). The IT Crowd: How Technology is Helping Children in Care. Children and Young People Now – Special Report Technology in Care. http://www.cypnow.co.uk/cyp/feature/1145511/crowd-technology-helping-children-care, date accessed 1 May 2015.

Gamache, P. (2002). 'University Students as Creators of Personal Knowledge: an alternative epistemological view', *Teaching in Higher Education*, vol. 7, no. 3, pp. 277–294.

General Social Care Council. (2002). *Accreditation of Universities to Grant Degrees in Social Work*. London: General Social Care Council.

Gibbs, G. (1988). *Learning by Doing: A Guide to Teaching and Learning Methods*. Further Education Unit.

Gibson, M. (2012). 'Narrative Practice and Social Work Education: Using a Narrative Approach in Social Work Practice Education to Develop Struggling Social Work Students', *Practice* (09503153), vol. 24, no. 1, pp. 53–65.

Gilbert, A. & Sliep, Y. (2009). 'Reflexivity in the Practice of Social Action: From Self- to Inter-relational Reflexivity', *South African Journal of Psychology*, vol. 39, no. 4, pp. 468–479.

Gitterman, A. (2004). 'Interactive Andragogy: Principles, Methods, and Skills', *Journal of Teaching in Social Work*, vol. 24, no. 3–4, pp. 95–112.

Goldkind, L. & Wolf, L. (2014). 'A Digital Environment Approach: Four Technologies That Will Disrupt Social Work Practice', *Social Work*, vol. 60, no. 1, pp. 85–87.

Goleman, D. (2004a). *Emotional Intelligence. Why it can matter more than IQ* (Vol. Omnibus edn). London: Bloomsbury.

Goleman, D. (2004b). *Working with Emotional Intelligence* (Vol. Omnibus edn). London: Bloomsbury.

Grant, L. & Kinman, G. (2013). '"Bouncing Back?" Personal Representations of Resilience of Student and Experienced Social Workers', *Practice* (09503153), vol. 25, no. 5, pp. 349–366.

Grant, L. & Kinman, G. (2014). *Developing Resilience for Social Work Practice*. London: Palgrave.
Grant, L. & Rutsch, E. (2013). How to build a culture of empathy with social work. http://www.youtube.com/watch?v=Wjysk9Ul7f4, date accessed 30 January 2014.
Grint, K. (2008). 'Wicked Problems and Clumsy Solutions: The Role of Leadership, Clinical Leader', in S. Brookes and K. Grint (eds), *The New Public Leadership Challenge*. Basingstoke and New York: Palgrave Macmillan, pp. 169–186.
Grotberg, E. H. (1995). A Guide to Promoting Resilience in Children: Strengthening the Human Spirit, http://resilnet.uiuc.edu/library/grotb95b.html, date accessed 1 May 2015.
Gursansky, D., Quinn, D. & Le Sueur, E. (2010). 'Authenticity in Reflection: Building Reflective Skills for Social Work', *Social Work Education*, vol. 29, no. 7, pp. 778–791.
GWI (2014). Global Device Summary Q3, https://www.globalwebindex.net/, date accessed 1 May 2015.
Hair, H. (2013). 'The Purpose and Duration of Supervision, and the Training and Discipline of Supervisors: What Social Workers Say They Need to Provide Effective Services', *British Journal of Social Work*, vol. 43, no. 8, pp. 1562–1588.
Hawkins, P. & Shohet, R. (2007). *Supervision in the Helping Professions*. Oxford: Open University Press.
HCPC (2012a). *Continuing Professional Development and your Registration*. London: Health and Care Professions Council.
HCPC (2012b). *Standards of Proficiency. Social Work in England*. London: Health and Care Professions Council.
Health and Care Professions Council (2012). Focus on Standards: Social Networking Sites, http://www.hcpc-uk.org/Assets/documents/100035B7Social_media_guidance.pdf, date accessed 1 May 2015.
Hodkinson, P., Biesta, G. & James, D. (2008). 'Understanding Learning Culturally: Overcoming the Dualism Between Social and Individual Views of Learning', *Vocations and Learning*, vol. 1, no. 1, pp. 27–47.
Howe, D. (2008). *The Emotionally Intelligent Social Worker*. Basingstoke: Palgrave Macmillan.
Howe, D. (2009). *A Brief Introduction to Social Work Theory*. Basingstoke: Palgrave Macmillan.
HSE (2008). Working Together to Reduce Stress at Work: A Guide for Employees, http://www.hse.gov.uk/pubns/indg424.pdf, date accessed 1 December 2014. Health and Safety Executive. Crown Copyright.
HSE (2014a). Signs and Symptoms. http://www.hse.gov.uk/stress/furtheradvice/signsandsymptoms.htm, date accessed 16 January 2015.
HSE (2014b). Stress-related and Psychological Disorders in Great Britain 2014, http://www.hse.gov.uk/statistics/causdis/stress/stress.pdf, date accessed 8 December 2014. Health and Safety Executive. Crown copyright.

Hyder, E. (2013). *Reading Groups, Libraries and Social Inclusion: Experiences of Blind and Partially Sighted People*. Reading: Ashgate Publishing Limited.
Illeris, K. (2002). *The Three Dimensions of Learning: Contemporary Learning Theory in the Tension Field Between the Cognitive, the Emotional and the Social*. Frederiksberg: Roskilde University Press; Leicester: Niace Publications.
Illeris, K. (2014a). 'Transformative Learning and Identity', *Journal of Transformative Education*, vol. 12, no. 2.
Illeris, K. (2014b). 'Transformative Learning Re-defined: As Changes in Elements of the Identity', *International Journal of Lifelong Education*, vol. 33, no. 5, pp. 573–586.
Ingram, R. (2013). 'Locating Emotional Intelligence at the Heart of Social Work Practice', *British Journal of Social Work*, vol. 43, no. 5, pp. 987–1004.
Ingram, R. (2015). *Understanding Emotions in Social Work: Theory, Practice and Reflection*. Berkshire: McGraw-Hill Education, Open University Press.
IRISS (2015). http://www.iriss.org.uk/, date accessed 1 May 2015.
Jack, G. & Donnellan, H. (2010). 'Recognising the Person Within the Developing Professional: Tracking the Early Careers of Newly Qualified Child Care Social Workers in Three Local Authorities in England', *Social Work Education*, vol. 29, no. 3, pp. 305–318.
Jahrami, H., Marnoch, G. & Gray, A. M. (2009). 'Use of Card Sort Methodology in the Testing of a Clinical Leadership Competencies Model', *Health Services Management Research*, vol. 22, no. 4, pp. 176–183.
JISC (2015). Developing Students Digital Literacy, http://www.jisc.ac.uk/guides/developing-students-digital-literacy, date accessed 1 May 2015.
Kadushin, D. & Harkness, A. (2014). *Supervision in Social Work* (5th edn). New York: Columbia University Press.
Kearns, S. & McArdle, K. (2012). 'Doing it Right?' – Accessing the Narratives of Identity of Newly Qualified Social Workers Through the Lens of Resilience: 'I am, I have, I can', *Child & Family Social Work*, vol. 17, no. 4, pp. 385–394.
Kellaway, K. (2013). 'Stories are our way of coping, of creating shape out of mess', *The Guardian* [online] 23 June 2013, http://www.theguardian.com/film/2013/jun/23/sarah-polley-stories-we-tell-interview, date accessed 5 February 2013.
Kelleher, N. (2015). *Does ASYE Work?* Paper presented at the National Organisation of Practice Teaching: Focus on Assessment, University of Salford.
Kerka, S. (2002). 'Journal Writing as an Adult Learning Tool', Practice Application Brief No. 22, Educational Resources Information Centre (ERIC), 22.
Kimball, E. & Kim, J. (2013). 'Virtual Boundaries: Ethical Considerations for the Use of Social Media in Social Work', *Social Work*, vol. 58, no. 2, pp. 185–188.

King, T. (2003). *The Truth About Stories: A Native Narrative*. Toronto, Ontario, Canada: House of Anansi Press. Oxford Universities Press. (2015) Oxford Dictionaries. http://www.oxforddictionaries.com/definition/english/dialectical, date accessed 30 January 2015.

Kinman, G. & Grant, L. (2011). 'Exploring Stress Resilience in Trainee Social Workers: The Role of Emotional and Social Competencies', *British Journal of Social Work*, vol. 41, no. 2, pp. 261–275.

Kinman, G. & Grant, L. (2012). Emotional Resilience in Social Work, http://www.communitycare.co.uk/emotional-resilience-expert-guide/, date accessed 23 August 2012.

Kinman, G., McMurray, I. & Williams, J. (2014). 'Enhancing Self-Knowledge, Coping Skills and Stress Resistance', in L. Grant & G. Kinman (eds), *Developing Resilience for Social Work Practice*. London: Palgrave.

Klein, M. (1997). *Envy and Gratitude and Other Works 1946–1963*. London: Vintage.

Knowles, M. S. (1984). *Andragogy in Action*. San Francisco and London: Jossey-Bass.

Knowles, M. S., Holton, E. & Swanson, R. A. (1998). *The Adult Learner: The Definitive Classic in Adult Education and Human Resource Development* (5th edn). Woburn, MA: Butterworth-Heinemann.

Kolb, D. (1984). *Experiential Learning*. Englewood Cliffs: NJ, Prentice Hall.

Lafferty, J. (2015). Social Times: Young People More Likely to Use Social Media in Developing Countries, http://www.adweek.com/socialtimes/study-young-people-more-likely-to-use-social-media-in-developing-countries/617242, date accessed 1 May 2015.

Lancaster, Y. P. (2006). *RAMPS: A Framework for Listening to Children*. London: Daycare Trust.

Larkins, C., Westwood, J. L., Berry, V. & Stone, C. (2014). 'A new sense of excitement about future prospects', The Reporters' Academy Paul Hamlyn Project Evaluation – Year 1. Preston: University of Central Lancashire.

Larrison, T. E. (2010). 'Capturing the Space in-between: Understanding the Relevance of Professional "Use of Self" for Social Work Education and Practice through Hermeneutic Phenomenology', *National Symposium on Doctoral Research in Social Work*, date accessed 9 December 2013.

Larrison, T. E. & Korr, W. S. (2013). 'Does Social Work Have a Signature Pedagogy?' *Journal of Social Work Education*, vol. 49, no. 2, pp. 194–206.

Learning Pool (2014). Understanding Child Development for 0–6 years, https://itunes.apple.com/gb/app/understanding-child-development/id721681546?mt=8, date accessed 1 May 2015.

Liquid Personnel & Munro, E. (2015). *The Social Work Survey 2014–2015*. Manchester: Liquid Personnel.

Lishman, J. (2007). *Handbook for Practice Learning in Social Work and Social Care* (2nd edn). London: Jessica Kingsley.

MacKenzie, S. K. & Wolf, M. M. (2012). 'Layering Sel(f)ves: Finding Acceptance, Community and Praxis through Collage', *Qualitative Report*, 17.

Maclean, S. & Harrison, R. (2015). *Social Work Theory: A Straightforward Guide for Practice Educators and Placement Supervisors*. Staffordshire: Kirwin Maclean.

Manthorpe, J., Moriarty, J., Hussein, S., Stevens, M. & Sharpe, E. (2015). 'Content and Purpose of Supervision in Social Work Practice in England: Views of Newly Qualified Social Workers, Managers and Directors', *British Journal of Social Work*, vol. 45, pp. 52–68.

Masters, A. (2006). *Stuart – A Life Backwards*. London: Harper Perennial Publishing.

Mayer, J. D., Salovey, P. & Caruso, D. R. (2004). 'Emotional Intelligence: Theory, Findings, and Implications', *Psychological Inquiry*, vol. 15, no. 3, pp. 197–215.

Mayer, J. D., Caruso, D. R., Panter, A. T. & Salovey, P. (2012). 'The Growing Significance of Hot Intelligences', *American Psychologist*, vol. 67, no. 6, pp. 502–503.

McEwan, I. (2014). *The Children Act*. London: Jonathan Cape Ltd.

McFadden, P. (2015). Measuring burnout among UK social workers: A Community Care study. http://www.communitycare.co.uk/2015/07/14/social-workers-on-the-edge-of-burnout-but-still-achieving-positive-changes/, date accessed 1 May 2015.

McNay, L. (1994). *Foucault: A Critical Introduction*. Cambridge: Polity.

Megele, C. (2015). *Psychosocial and Relationship-based Practice*. Northwich: Critical Publishing.

Meyer, C. F., Depraetere, I. & Langford, C. (2012). *Advanced English Grammar: A Linguistic Approach*. London: Bloomsbury.

Miller, G. & Fox, K. J. (2004). Building Bridges: The Possibility of Analytic Dialogue Between Ethnography, Conversation Analysis and Foucault', in D. Silverman (ed.), *Qualitative Research: Theory, Method and Practice* (2nd edn). London: SAGE.

Milner, J. & O'Byrne, P. (2002). *Assessment in Social Work* (2nd edn). Basingstoke: Palgrave Macmillan.

Morgan, D. (2012). *Disappearing Home*. Birmingham: Tindal Street Press.

Morrison, T. (2005). *Supervision in Social Care: Making a Real Difference for Staff and Service Users*. Brighton: Pavilion.

Morrison, T. (2007). 'Emotional Intelligence, Emotion and Social Work: Context, Characteristics, Complications and Contribution', *British Journal of Social Work*, vol. 37, no. 2, pp. 245–263.

Morley, C. (2013). 'Using Critical Reflection to Research Possibilities for Change', *British Journal of Social Work, Advance Access*, published February 13.

Mortiboys, A. (2011). *How to Be an Effective Teacher in Higher Education: Answers to Lecturers' Questions*. Berkshire: Open University Press.

Mulder, C. & Aubrey, D. (2014). 'Facilitating Self-Reflection: The Integration of Photovoice in Graduate Social Work Education', *Social Work Education*, vol. 33, no. 8, pp. 1017–1036.

Mumm, A. M. (2006). 'Teaching Social Work Students Practice Skills', *Journal of Teaching in Social Work*, vol. 26, no. 3/4, pp. 71–89.

Munro, E. (2002). *Effective Child Protection*. London: SAGE.

Munro, E. (2011). *Munro Review of Child Protection: Final Report. A Child-centred System*. London.

Narey, M. (2014). Making the Education of Social Workers Consistently Effective, *Department for Education*, www.gov.uk/government/publications, date accessed 1 May 2015.

Neenan, M. & Dryden, W. (2008). *Life Coaching: A Cognitive Behavioural Approach* London: Routledge.

Nelson-Jones, R. (1993). *Practical Counselling and Helping Skills*. London: Cassell.

NHS. (2014). Cognitive behavioural therapy (CBT) – How it works, http://www.nhs.uk/Conditions/Cognitive-behavioural-therapy/Pages/How-does-it-work.aspx, date accessed 26 January 2015.

NISCC (2002). Northern Ireland Social Care Council Codes of Practice, http://www.niscc.info/social-worker, date accessed 1 May 2015.

OED (2015). Oxford English Dictionary, http://www.oed.com/, date accessed 3 July 2015.

Oko, J. (2011). *Understanding and Using Theory in Social Work* (2nd edn). Exeter: Learning Matters.

Parker, J. (2006). 'Developing Perceptions of Competence during Practice Learning', *British Journal of Social Work*, vol. 36, no. 6, pp. 1017–1036.

Parker, J. (2007). 'Developing Effective Practice Learning for Tomorrow's Social Workers', *Social Work Education*, vol. 26, no. 8, pp. 763–779.

Parrott, H. & Cherry, E. (2011). 'Using Structured Reading Groups to Facilitate Deep Learning', *Teaching Sociology*, vol. 39, no. 4, pp. 354–370.

Payne, M. (2011). 'Risk, Security and Resilience Work in Social Work Practice', *Social Work Review / Revista de Asistenta Sociala*, no. 1, pp. 7–14.

Peebles, S. (2013). *Snake Road*. London: Chatto & Windus Publisher.

Petrosky, A. (1986). 'Critical Thinking: Qu'est-Ce Que C'est?', *The English Record*, vol. 37, no. 3, pp. 2–5.

Prensky, M. (2001). Digital Natives, Digital Immigrants, *On the Horizon*, vol. 9, no. 5, http://www.marcprensky.com/writing/Prensky%20-%20Digital%20Natives,%20Digital%20Immigrants%20-%20Part1.pdf, date accessed 11 June 2015.

Pritchard, A. (2014). *Ways of Learning: Learning Theories and Learning Styles in the Classroom* (3rd edn). Oxfordshire, England and New York: Routledge.

Pullman, P. (2011). 'Imaginary Friends', *New Statesman*, vol. 140, no. 5084, pp. 74–77.
Raider, P. (2003). Socratic Seminars: Creating a Community of Inquiry. Sponsored by Greater Rochester Teacher Center Network, June, 2003, http://www.greececsd.org/files/filesystem/GRTCN_Socratic_Seminars.pdf, date accessed 1 May 2015.
Rajan-Rankin, S. (2014). 'Self-Identity, Embodiment and the Development of Emotional Resilience', *British Journal of Social Work*, vol. 44, no. 8, pp. 2426–2442.
Riener, C. & Willingham, D. (2010). 'The Myth of Learning Styles', *Change*, vol. 42, no. 5, pp. 32–35.
Riessman, C. K. (2001). 'Analysis of Personal Narratives', in J. F. Gubrium & J. A. Holstein (eds), *Handbook of Interview Research*. Thousand Oaks: SAGE.
Rogers, A. G. (1996). *Shining Affliction: A Story of Harm and Healing in Psychotherapy*. London: Penguin Books Ltd.
Rogers, C. R. (2004). *On Becoming a Person*. London: Constable and Company Ltd.
Romeo, L. (2015). Tweeting is Teaching. 11 February, Lyn Romeo Blog, https://lynromeo.blog.gov.uk/2015/02/11/tweeting-is-teaching/, date accessed 9 June 2015.
Rosen, A. (1992). 'Community Psychiatric Services: Will They Endure?', *Current Opinion in Psychiatry*, vol. 5, pp. 257–265.
Rosenthal, N. (2012). '10 Ways to Enhance Your Emotional Intelligence', https://www.psychologytoday.com/blog/your-mind-your-body/201201/10-ways-enhance-your-emotional-intelligence, date accessed 20 March 2015.
Rowling, J. K. (2013). *The Casual Vacancy*. London: The Little Brown Book Group.
Saarni, C. (2000). 'Emotional Competence. A Developmental Perspective', in R. Bar-On & J. D. A. Parker (eds), *Handbook of Emotional Intelligence: The Theory and Practice of Development, Evaluation, Education, and Implementation – At Home, School, and in the Workplace*. San Francisco, CA: Jossey-Bass.
Salovey, P. & Mayer, J. D. (1989). 'Emotional Intelligence', *Imagination, Cognition and Personality*, vol. 9, no. 3, pp. 185–211.
Sapey, R. (1997). Social Work Tomorrow: Towards a Critical Understanding of Technology in Social Work', *British Journal of Social Work*, vol. 27, pp. 803–814.
Sapphire (1997). *Push*. New York: Knopf Doubleday Publishing Group.
Schön, D. A. (1991). *The Reflective Practitioner: How Professionals Think in Action*. Aldershot: Ashgate.
Scourfield, J. & Taylor, A. (2013). 'Using a Book Group to Facilitate Student Learning About Social Work. Social Work Education', *The International Journal*, vol. 32.

Seigel, D. J. (2007). *The Mindful Brain*. New York: Norton.
Senge, P. (1990). *The Fifth Discipline: The Art and Practice of the Learning Organisation*. New York: Doubleday.
Shulman, L. (1999). *The Skills of Helping Individuals, Families, Groups, and Communities* (4th edn). Itasca, IL: F. E. Peacock Publishers, Inc.
Singh Cooner, T. (2013). Social Work Social Media App, https://itunes.apple.com/gb/app/social-work-social-media/id656114442?mt=8, date accessed 1 May 2015.
Slater, P. (2007). 'The Passing of the Practice Teaching Award: History, Legacy, Prospects', *Social Work Education*, vol. 26, no. 8, pp. 749–762.
Smith, R. (2008). *Social Work and Power*. Basingstoke: Palgrave Macmillan.
Sousa, D. A. (2011). *How the Brain Learns* (4th edn). Thousand Oaks, CA: Corwin Press.
Starr, J. (2008). *The Coaching Manual: The Definitive Guide to the Process, Principles and Skills of Personal Coaching*. Harlow: Pearson.
Statista (2015). The Statistics Portal, http://www.statista.com/statistics/272014/global-social-networks-ranked-by-number-of-users/, date accessed 1 May 2015.
Stevenson, O. (2013). *Reflections on a Life in Social Work: A Personal & Professional Memoir*. Buckingham: Hinton House Publishers.
Stone, C. (2014). *An Exploration of How Practice Educators Use Competency Frameworks to Assess Social Work Students in Practice Learning Settings*. University of Central Lancashire, Doctoral Thesis.
Stone, C., Malihi-Shoja, L., McKeown, M. & COMENSUS (2013). 'Service User Involvement', in A. Worsley, T. Mann, A. Olsen & E. Mason-Whitehead (eds), *Key Concepts in Social Work Practice*. London: SAGE.
SWRB (2012). 'Standards for Employers of Social Workers in England and Supervision Framework', http://www.tcsw.org.uk/uploadedFiles/TheCollege/_CollegeLibrary/Reform_resources/standards-for-employers(em1).pdf, date accessed 1 May 2015.
SWTF (2009). 'Building a Safe, Confident Future', the Final Report of the Social Work Task Force.
Taylor, A. (2013). The Use of Book Groups in Social Work Education, https://storify.com/AMLTaylor66/the-use-of-book-clubs-in-social-work-education, date accessed 14 February 2015.
Taylor, A. (2014a). 'When Actual Meets Virtual: Social Work Book Groups as a Teaching and Learning Medium in Social Work Education', in J. Westwood (ed.), *Social Media in Social Work Education*. Hertfordshire: Critical Publishing.
Taylor, A. (2014b). The Social Work Book Group: Using Fiction to Support Learning. *The Guardian*, http://www.theguardian.com/social-care-network/social-life-blog/2014/jun/06/social-work-book-group, date accessed 23 February 2015.

Taylor, A. (2015). 'Fiction, Book Groups and Social Work Education', in G. Brewer & R. Hogarth (eds), *Creative Education, Teaching and Learning: Creativity, Engagement and the Student Experience*. Basingstoke: Palgrave Macmillan.

Taylor, B. & Devine, T. (1993). *Assessing Needs and Planning Care in Social Work*. Aldershot: Ashgate.

Taylor, E. W. & Laros, A. (2014). Researching the Practice of Fostering Transformative Learning: Lessons Learned from the Study of Andragogy. *Journal of Transformative Education*, vol. 12, no. 2.

The College of Social Work (2013). The Professional Capabilities Framework, The College of Social Work, http://www.collegeofsocialwork .org/, date accessed 1 May 2015.

Thompson, L. J. & West, D. (2013). 'Professional Development in the Contemporary Educational Context: Encouraging Practice Wisdom', *Social Work Education*, vol. 32, no. 1, pp. 118–133. Thompson, N. (1993). *Anti-Discriminatory Practice*. London: Palgrave Macmillan.

Thompson, N. (2013). 'The Emotionally Competent Professional', in J. Parker & M. Doel (eds), *Professional Social Work*. Exeter: Learning Matters.

Thompson, N. & Thompson, S. (2015). *The Social Work Companion*. London: Palgrave Macmillan.

Thresher, K., Boreham, L., Dennison, L., Owen, C., Smith, L. & Scallan, S. (2013). 'Exploring Art with Foundation Doctors: Reflecting on Clinical Experience', *Education for Primary Care*, vol. 24, no. 3, pp. 212–215.

Trevithick, P. (2005). *Social Work Skills: A Practice Handbook* (2nd edn). Maidenhead: Open University Press.

Trigell, J. (2004). *Boy A*. London: Serpents Tail Publisher.

Triggs, S. (2015). 'Social Care Book Club: "These conversations are really powerful in helping us to reflect"', *Community Care*, http://www. communitycare.co.uk/2015/04/08/social-care-book-club-conversations- really-powerful-helping-us-reflect/, date accessed 15 May 2015.

Urdang, E. (2010). 'Awareness of Self – A Critical Tool', *Social Work Education*, vol. 29, no. 5, pp. 523–538.

Vejar, C. (2008). *Critical Thinking: An Academic Perspective. Research Starters Education*. Ipswich, MA: Research Starters.

Walker, H. (2008). *Studying For Your Social Work Degree*. Exeter: Learning Matters.

Walker, J., Crawford, K. & Parker, J. (2008). *Practice Education in Social Work: A Handbook for Practice Teachers, Assessors and Educators*. Exeter: Learning Matters.

Wenger, E. (2000). *Communities of Practice: Learning, Meaning, and Identity*. Cambridge: Cambridge University Press.

Wernersbach, B., Crowley, S., Bates, S. & Rosenthal, C. (2014). 'Study Skills Course Impact on Academic Self-Efficacy', *Journal of Developmental Education*, vol. 37, no. 3, pp. 14–33.

Whatis.com? (2015). Definition: Digital Divide, http://whatis.techtarget.com/definition/digital-divide, date accessed 15 June 2015.

White, D. S. & Le Cornu, A. (2011). Visitors and Residents: A New Typology for Online Engagement, 5 September 2011, *First Monday*, http://firstmonday.org/ojs/index.php/fm/article/view/3171/3049, date accessed 10 June 2015.

White, S., Fook, J. & Gardner, F. (2006). *Critical reflection in health and social care*. Maidenhead: Open University Press.

Wilks, S. E. & Spivey, C. A. (2010). 'Resilience in Undergraduate Social Work Students: Social Support and Adjustment to Academic Stress', *Social Work Education*, vol. 29, no. 3, pp. 276–288.

Williams, S. & Rutter, L. (2010). *The Practice Educator's Handbook*. Exeter: Learning Matters.

Wilson, G. (2013). 'Evidencing Reflective Practice in Social Work Education: Theoretical Uncertainties and Practical Challenges', *British Journal of Social Work*, vol. 43, no. 1, pp. 154–172.

Winterson, J. (2012). *Why Be Happy When You Can Be Normal*. New York: Grove Press.

Wodlinger, M. (2007). *Adult Education*. Maitland: Xulon.

Wonnacott, J. (2012). *Mastering Social Work Supervision*. London: Jessica Kingsley.

INDEX

Adult learning theory (*see* learning theory)
Assessed and Supported Year in Employment (ASYE) *see also* Newly Qualified Social Workers
ASYE programmes, 5, 14, 20–22

Book group and fiction, 168–180
  dialectical journaling, 173, 176–178
  recommended reading list, 179
burnout, 15, 52, 66–70, 79 (*see also* stress)

Capability for social work
  concerns about capability for the profession 2, 8, 14, 106
career development and career advancement, 45–48
  see also CPD
caseload, (*see* workload)
coaching, 122–134
  emotional intelligence and coaching, 124–125 (*see also* emotional intelligence)
  emotional vocabulary for coaching, 130–132
  difficult situations and powerful questions in coaching, 125–126
  ACRON model, 126, 129–130, 131
  visualisation in coaching, 132–134

competence (*see* capability)
continuing professional development (CPD)
  career development and career advancement, 45–48
  employers responsibility, 5
  recording of continuing professional development, 42–43
  requirement to undertake continuing professional development, 1–8, 12, 14–15, 20, 23, 29, 83–84, 169
CPD, (*see* continuing professional development)
critical reflection, 96–104 (*see also* reflection)

Dialectical journaling (*see* book group)
digitalisation and digital competence
  Apps using in practice, 162
  Apps for learning, 163–164
  conduct in using digital platforms, 159–160
  digital and social media resources, 165–166
  digital competence and digital literacy, 156–163
  Facebook group for foster carers, 164
  mapping use of technology, 160–162

digitalisation and digital
    competence – *continued*
  social networking sites, 155
  virtual learning environment, 156
  Web 2.0, 156

Emotional intelligence, 6, 50–64
  coaching and emotional
    intelligence, 124–125
  developing emotional
    intelligence, 53–64
  emotional labour, 52
  emotional vocabulary, 130–132
  supervision and emotional
    intelligence, 63, 115
employer responsibilities
  for CPD, 5
  for supervision, 106
  in relation to resilience, 70

Feedback, 34, 48, 55, 60, 84–85, 98,
  111, 115–116, 138–142, 147–152
  Service user feedback, (*see*
    service users and carers)
fiction (*see* book group)

HCPC (Health and Care Professions
  Council)
  requirement to undertake
    continuing professional
    development, 5
  HCPC and supervision, 106

Initial social work education
  programmes (*see* social work
  education)

Knowledge
  forms of knowledge, 19, 29–30

Learning methods and learning
  theory, 24–49
  andragogy, 52–30, 43

behaviour modification, 31–32
book group methodology,
  (*see* book group)
card sort, 38–40
constructive alignment, 33–34, 43
challenges to learning, 48–49
cognition within learning,
  32–33, 77–79
cognitive behaviour theory,
  77–79
deep learning, 28–29 (*see also*
  surface learning)
digital competence (*see*
  digitalisation and digital
  competence)
feedback and learning (*see*
  feedback)
learning about and learning
  from service users, 135–153
learning agreements, 43–45
learning styles, 35–37
learning taxonomy, 34–35
modelling, 32, 37–38, 69–70, 108
motivation to learn, 25–29, 49
narrative methodology, 96–104
neurolinguistics programming,
  133
other mediums for supporting
  learning, 40–41
recording learning (*see*
  continuing professional
  development)
reflective learning (*see* reflection)
reflective supervision (*see*
  supervision)
role models (*see* modelling)
social learning theory, 31–32
surface learning, 28 (*see also*
  deep learning)
transformative learning theory
  and transformative change,
  24–49
visualisation, 132–134

Modelling, 32, 37–38, 69–70, 108
Motivation to learn, 25–29, 49

Newly qualified social worker (*see also* Assessed and Supported Year in Employment)
  newly qualified social workers need to grow and develop, 2–10, 11–15
  NQSW experiences including feeling overwhelmed, 4, 12, 67
  support for NQSW, 5, 14, 20–22, 107, 112, 120–121
  transition from student to social worker, 1–10, 11–23
NQSW (*see* newly qualified social workers)

Placements, 4, 6, 9, 12, 13, 16–17, 23, 45, 55, 67, 71–72, 98, 149, 163, 181–188
practice learning opportunities (*see* placements)
practice learning placements (*see* placements)
Practice Educators, 6–7, 55, 60, 71, 120–121
practice wisdom, 19, 29–30, 83–84, 193

Qualifying social work education (*see* social work education)

Reading groups (*see* book group)
reflection, 81–95
  critical reflection, 81–82, 96–104
  reflecting on a learning activity, 92–93
  reflective cycle, 15–17, 84, 86, 92, 117–118
  reflective learning plans, 94–95
  reflective writing, 85
  reflective questions, 90–92
  using art to reflect, 93–94
reflective learning (*see* reflection)
reflective practice (*see* reflection)
reflexivity, 81–82 (*see also* reflection)
resilience, 6, 23, 52, 65–80
  developing resilience, 12, 15, 65–80
  stress and resilience (*see* stress)
  self-efficacy and resilience, 68–71 (*see also* self-efficacy)
  supervision and resilience, 69–70
role models (*see* modelling)

Self-efficacy, 56, 60–63, 65, 68–71, 98
service users and carers
  feedback from service users and carers (*see* feedback)
  learning about and learning from service users, 135–153
social media (*see* digitalisation and digital competence)
social work education, 1–8, 11–23, 24, 28–30
  history of social work education, 2, 13–15
social work role, 5, 14–17, 47–48, 72, 87–90, 11–112, 114, 118–119, 167
  challenges of being a social worker, 11–13, 23, 50–53, 63–67, 79–80
stress, 12, 51–52, 65–67, 70, 72–77, 79, 107, 119
Stressors, 65
supervision, 105–121
  addressing anxieties in supervision, 119
  emotional intelligence in supervision (*see* emotional intelligence)

supervision – *continued*
   Morrison's 4x4x4 supervision model, 117–119
   observation and assessment of the workers capabilities within supervision, 115–116
   partnership and power in supervision, 116
   peer and group supervision, 120
   reflective questions for supervision, 118–119
   role clarity and supervision, 114
   supervisee's rights and responsibilities, 109–111
   supervision agenda, 112–114
   supervision contract, 111–112
   supervision history, 108–109
   supervision for reflective learning, 19, 35–36, 41–42, 57, 114–119
   supervisory relationship, 107–108

Transformative learning theory and transformative change, 24–49

Workload,
   management of workload, 12, 112–113
   demands of, 49, 66–67, 169